MYTH AND CHRISTIANITY

MYTH AND CHRISTIANITY

An inquiry into the possibility of religion

without myth

by Karl Jaspers and Rudolf Bultmann

The Noonday Press : New York

A division of

Farrar, Straus & Giroux

TRANSLATOR'S NOTE

This book was published in German under the title, *Die Frage der Entmythologisierung*. The essay, "Myth and Religion" by Dr. Jaspers, served as the basis for a lecture delivered by him at a Congress of Swiss Theologians at Basel. It was later published in *Schweizerische theologische Bundschau* (1953) and in a German monthly, *Merkur*. Professor Bultmann's reply first appeared in *Theologische Zeitschrift,* published by the Faculty of Theology of the University of Basel (vol. 10, fasc. 2, March–April 1954). Dr. Jaspers' rejoinder was first published as an open letter in *Merkur*.

CONTENTS

MYTH AND CHRISTIANITY

1
MYTH AND RELIGION

By Karl Jaspers

BACKGROUND OF THE DISCUSSION

No philosophy can comprehend religion either as a historical phenomenon or as a living faith. Philosophic thinking confronts religion as an ever-perplexing ultimate, a weight it cannot lift, or a resistance it cannot surmount. When, occasionally, it seems to us that the resistance has been surmounted, we do not experience the gratification produced by the discovery of a truth; rather, we feel something like terror, as before a sudden void.

That is why I begin my lecture with some hesitation. I am to speak of a world in which I am not at home, of which I have no right to speak by virtue of practice or office. Beside the theologian's, my learning is inadequate. Nor am I sufficiently informed about contemporary religious movements. Here I am like a traveler in a foreign country, looking at things from the outside. My only hope is that here, too, an outsider may notice things which the native misses, but which are nonetheless important.

And yet, a sense of inadequacy remains. I venture to speak to you, since you have asked me, but the fact remains that the philosopher should not interfere in the affairs of the minister or the theologian. What happened to Hegel and to Schelling is a sufficient warning.

However, today we are faced with a peculiar situation. Bultmann's views on the demythologization of religion, which have aroused widespread and lively discussions, have assumed the proportions of an event touching the very essence of religion. This alone is enough to shake the philosopher out of his aloofness, even though the question is outside his field. But there is more. Bultmann's ideas evolve within the sphere of philosophy (up to a point that will be named later), and hence are subject to philosophical criticism. For both these reasons philosophical discussion is indicated. Since I run the risk of trespassing on others' territories, I hope you will permit me to make assertions which in view of the restricted scale of this lecture, will not be supported fully. However, the issues under discussion do most seriously concern my philosophizing.

I. TWO WEAK PREMISES

Bultmann's demand for the demythologizing of religion is based on two premises. The first is his conception of modern science and of the modern view of the world, which leads him to negate many articles of the Christian faith. The second is his conception of philosophy, which enables him to give an existentialist interpretation to certain contents of faith, that, in his opinion, are still true. He thinks that such an interpretation derives from scientific philosophy. These premises are the main pillars upon which his argument is built. These pillars seem to me not strong enough to bear its weight.

1. *Modern Science and the Modern View of the World*

Bultmann speaks of a modern view of the world which asserts a self-contained causality and tolerating no miraculous intervention. He speaks also of the modern view of man, which asserts mankind's unity against the alleged intrusions of gods and demons from outside. Finally, he speaks of the principles of scientific method, characterized by testing and verification. What does he mean by this?

Has Bultmann in mind a certain mode of thinking that is overwhelmingly current today and that is the distinguishing characteristic of modern man? It scarcely seems possible. The Resurrection, for instance, was just as implausible to the contemporaries of Jesus as it is to modern man. To exaggerate the spiritual differences between one age and another leads to overlooking the identical elements that characterize man as such. Thus, materialism and a naturalistic realism have always been with us; similarly, man's disposition to believe in the absurd is as unchanged as ever, no less strong today than it was then. It is only the contents of this faith in the absurd that are partly new: for example, belief in the advent of a definitive happiness for all in a classless society magically brought to birth through violence. This modern belief is analogous to the early missionary faith that the Kingdom of God will be realized simultaneously with the end of the world at the moment when the Gospel shall have been preached to all mankind (as the Bible prophesies). The absurd faiths of the modern era, ranging from astrology to theosophy, and from National Socialism to Bolshevism, suggest that superstition has no less power over the human mind today than it had formerly. Such permanent elements of human nature are universal, and have nothing to do with modern science, no more than with similarly permanent elements of rationality. Absurd modern faiths may very well make occasional use of scientific results, without grasping their origin or meaning.

Or does Bultmann have in mind modern science proper, which is actually something new in history, having begun in the late Middle Ages, although its realization dates only from the eighteenth century? This science, however, whose name is invoked by everyone, is known to surprisingly few: indeed, there are many scholars, and Bultmann, a serious historian, is apparently one of them, who are unfamiliar with its principles. A crucial feature of modern science is that it does not provide a total world-view, because it recognizes that this is impossible. It was science that liberated us from total views of the world, and for the first time in history. All previous epochs (and even our own at the level of the average man) have clung to general conceptions of this kind. Because it takes seriously the principles of cogent, universal, and systematic knowledge, science is always aware of its limitations, understands the particularity of its insights, and knows that it nowhere explores Being, but only objects in the world. It studies these methodically, aware of its boundaries at any given moment, and of its inability to provide guidance in life. Modern science has developed the new knowledge, which the ancient Greeks foreshadowed in their mathematics, medicine, geography, astronomy, mechanics, and political thought, failing to attain a general and basic scientific approach for lack of patient and systematic co-operation. In consequence of this development, the insights achieved by scientific method are available to, and are accepted as valid by all men everywhere who can grasp them. No earlier rationalistic system, no philosophy, was ever as successful in this respect as modern science has been, with its methodology and specialization. But where questions of faith are concerned, the impact of modern science is no more disintegrating than that of the universal rationalisms of earlier times. Only a basic misunderstanding of modern science, such as is very common today even among specialized researchers, leads to such a conclusion. Down to the present, this science has been accessible to the masses only in the form of final results referring to the totality of things, a form that absolutizes and distorts the actual results of science, giving rise to spuriously scientific total views. These reflect modern scientific superstition rather than real knowledge or insight into the meaning, content, and boundaries of science.

When Bultmann speaks of modern science, he uses various traditional expressions, in a fairly summary way. For instance, he refers to mythical and scientific thinking as mere contraries, and he says that scientific thinking is prefigured in operational thinking. In each instance, he has hit on a partial truth. But he completely misses the meaning of modern science when he asserts that scientific thinking arose out of the Greek search for the *arché*, or the principle that introduces unity into the manifold. This question was and remains a philosophical question; science cannot ask it methodologically, nor can it answer it. Only systematic theories are scientific: they are built on assumptions which are always hypothetical, and are guided by unifying ideas which can never bear upon the whole of Being. Questions are scientific only when they indicate starting points for genuine methodological investigations. Bultmann's statement, "The unity of the world in scientific thinking is matched by the unity of scientific thinking itself" is completely false. The opposite is true.

2. *The Notion of a Scientific Philosophy*

According to Bultmann's premise, which reflects no more than the average rationalistic spirit of any epoch, science has destroyed a large number of Biblical beliefs. But Bultmann's purpose is not to destroy religion: he wants to rescue it. And he effects this rescue by means of what he calls "existentialist interpretation." For this he needs a philosophy, which he calls "scientific philosophy." In his opinion this scientific philosophy achieves a natural understanding of human existence, this empirical existence which is concerned about itself, which is oriented toward death in Fear and Care, which is finite and rootless, flung into the world without origin or destination, inherently precarious, and so on. About this philosophy professed by Bultmann, the following must be said:

(*a*) Bultmann bases himself explicitly and, in effect, exclusively, on Heidegger's book *Sein und Zeit*. Whether he understood this book in Heidegger's sense, is a matter for the philosopher to decide. To me, it seems that we are confronted with a peculiar situation. Heidegger's book is a complicated affair. In the form of an objective phenomenological analysis, he draws up a list of existentialist concepts, the so-called *Existentialia,* an analogy from the [Kantian] categories, and presents us with a doctrine as well knit and coherent as a steel structure. The whole is not motivated by the mere will to know reality as it is, but by *a* fundamental experience of human existence, not by *the* fundamental experience of human existence, in the sense of universally valid experience. Heidegger renounces all faith, taking up an attitude which in its openness to Nothingness appeals to "modern" men, and approaches Being with foreboding. This endows his construction with life and gravity.

This philosophy seems to me grounded in ambiguities. It operates with existential terms; in fact, it derives from Kierkegaard, Luther, and St. Augustine. But at the same time it operates scientifically, phenomenologically, objectively. The appeal to selfhood, to authenticity, and to actual being—a sinking into the original, historical facticity (*Sosein*), in order to be appropriated—the appeal to earnest questioning in a hopeless situation, is present as it is in the great philosophical tradition, though the ideas of that tradition tend to acquire a hollow sound. At the same time, Heidegger's thought is presented in objective terms, as a doctrine, and as a result it commits us no more than the traditional systems. What we have, then, is a noncommittal, phenomenological knowledge, and by the same token, a learnable, usable knowledge that is a perversion of philosophy. This is why psychiatrists were able to employ *Existentialia* to describe certain states of mental illness, both chronic and acute, often not without success. And this is also why Bultmann can employ the *Existentialia* as an alleged discovery of scientific philosophy, useful for the exegesis and appropriation of Biblical texts. Such a use of the *Existentialia* was made easier by the fact that they themselves originate in a thinking rooted in the Bible.

(*b*) Because Bultmann confines philosophy to one book by Heidegger, and, as I suspect, misunderstands that book when he emphasizes its "scientific," objective, scholastic aspect, he in effect cuts himself off from all philosophy. His writings reveal this in other ways as well. Whenever Bultmann refers to the history of philosophy in his studies, he is concerned with statements that can be quoted with the superficial correctness of historical data; he is not concerned with philosophy itself. He appears to be untouched by the least breath of Kantian or Platonic thinking. His conception of philosophy, which I believe foreign to Heidegger himself, is that of nineteenth-century academicians or Hellenistic doxographers. Heidegger himself would surely be surprised at any theology based upon it.

(*c*) If the various attempts at philosophizing which are today lumped together as Existentialism have anything in common despite their differences of tendency, form, and content, it is, negatively, the rejection of so-called scientific philosophy, and, positively, the affirmation of a moral earnestness foreign to mere knowing. Now, this state of affairs is veiled by a distinction which once again gives an opening to philosophical inauthenticity, namely, the distinction between existentialist analysis and existential thinking. I don't know whether Heidegger himself has drawn such a distinction—it would be in keeping with the ambiguities of his thought referred to above—or whether it was introduced by Bultmann. The consequences of this distinction are: Existentialist analysis seeks to formulate with scientific objectivity that which can have meaning only in terms of existential thinking; what was meant by the *Existentialia* only as a sign, an indication, is turned into a thing; what has meaning only as a summons to awaken, or a stimulus to unrest, is treated as universally valid cognition. What can be achieved only through inward commitment becomes a matter of noncommittal knowledge; responsibility for things said is confined to scientifically rational responsibility, instead of extending to inner meaning and consequences; thinkers take the liberty of speaking in the name of "abstract consciousness" where they are entitled to speak seriously only for themselves; an illusion of knowledge is created in matters where everything depends on the ground that is never known and that, since Kierkegaard, has been called *Existenz;* conceptual definitions congeal what only a transcending thinking can achieve step by step, each meaningful only to the degree that it evokes an inner resonance and becomes real in the actual life of the thinker.

Furthermore, this turning of signs into objective *Existentialia,* this concern for scientific philosophy, implies a new dogmatism, which is expressed less in concepts than in the general attitude: a modern mode of despair thus achieves self-understanding without transcendence. Resolution (*Entschlossenheit*) as such, without content, suffices unto itself. An alleged knowledge of what we are or can be or want to be or allegedly cannot help being, begets a new intellectual intolerance, presenting as universal truth that which is valid only for the thinker's own life, on the grounds that it is modern, of the age. The tendency of many rebels to absolutize their own rootlessness in nothingness originates in that false idea, not in any scientific advance by a scientific philosophy.

Bultmann, although he keeps aloof from the tendency we have just described, believes in such a "scientific philosophy." That is why he isolates the philosophic ideas contained in Heidegger's book *Sein und Zeit* and interprets them as a scientifical, universally valid insight into human existence. This interpretation may describe one incidental, though scarcely unequivocal, aspect of the book. Detached from its context and made noncommittal, this thinking becomes an instrument for the intellectual assimilation of existential propositions in the Bible by means of existentialist exegesis. It is a deceptive instrument. At all events, it makes one blind to philosophy. As for what it does to the Bible, I have my doubts. Why do things that have resonance in Heidegger sound so hollow in Bultmann? It seems to me the reason for this is Bultmann's scientific prejudice with regard to the possibilities of philosophy, his superstitious belief in a "scientific philosophy."

Existentialist analysis can never give scientific insight or replace moral earnestness. Existentialist analysis, when it is philosophical, is never neutral in the manner of science, is never universally valid, but is at the same time existential: it speaks out of moral earnestness with a view to commitment, out of deep emotion to arouse emotion. It speaks with a sense of responsibility, not for scientific correctness, which must not be sought and which cannot be found here, but for the truth of that which I will do and am, and in appeal to others to respond. Philosophical language is responsible for the goal of its thoughts, for that into which they transform me inwardly, and for the consequences that follow in external action, in concrete decisions, and in everyday life. I escape from commitment by the linguistic distinction between existentialist and existential. It is not a critical, clarifying distinction, but one that seduces into noncommitment. It paralyzes instead of awakening. It leads to endless talk, which does not advance. It gives a hollow tone to what is said.

II. BULTMANN'S VIEW OF TRANSCENDENTAL PHILOSOPHY

In thus venturing to characterize Bultmann's position as alien to both science and philosophy, have I not been guilty of exaggeration, to say the least? Has not philosophy still another task, which I have overlooked in my discussion so far, namely, the clarification and critical delimitation of all our modes of knowledge and belief? Actually, it is in this area that Bultmann tries to establish the possibility of faith with the help of his conception of myth and of the relation between knowledge and faith. This philosophical task bears upon the form, not the content, of the ideas involved. Demythologization, we are told, by exposing a historically obsolete form of thinking, which has become false, will liberate religion from that form. We are here entering the domain of philosophical investigation which was first explored by Plato, which since Kant has been called "transcendental," and which is today carried on in various ways, among others, by elucidating the modes of the Encompassing. Such transcendental reflection, as distinct from philosophical speculation proper, which discloses meaning, cannot be regarded as scientific in the full sense of the term, although it comes close to scientific cognition in so far as it claims universal validity.

Once again I shall confine myself to a few theses:

1. *Immediate Experience and the Modes of the Encompassing*

Everything that is real for us and that we really are, is present in immediate experience. But this immediate experience cannot be grasped in its moments of plenitude or impoverishment, in its vital concentration or dispersal—it cannot be grasped as a state at all. It remains the site of all actualization (*Verwirklichung*), yet it remains unknowable as a whole and as an object. But with regard to everything that is asserted, we raise the question whether and how its content is actual for us, a question which is answered not in terms of reason, but in terms of the given reality in this immediate experience. Without such an answer there is only empty talk.

In immediate experience a conscious mind is directed at objects which it sets before itself. All clarity, all thought and language, is in this split between the thinker and the thing he has in mind, between subject and object. This split is the luminous crest of a wave surging above unfathomable depths; it may also be compared to a flame that is nourished by the flow of the inexhaustible Encompassing. If the flow stops, if awareness of the deep ground is absent, if there is only the split between a conscious mind and the objects it intends, then we have no more than a rustle of withered leaves, the random swirling of dead husks of words, producing a semblance of external order and meaning in endless, arbitrary variation.

By various methods, philosophy seeks to comprehend the mind and its deep ground in the whole range of its potentialities. It sets up levels of cognition, from sensory knowledge to the super-sensory intuition of the godhead (antiquity and the Middle Ages), or it analyzes the faculties of the human soul, namely, the faculty of thinking as apprehension of objects, the faculty of the will as capacity for execution, and the faculty of feeling as awareness of psychic states (Kant), or it elucidates the modes of the Encompassing, within which the split between subject and object takes place. Such modes are empirical existence in an environment, abstract consciousness with its world of objects, the spirit with its world of forms, and *Existenz* with its transcendence. When philosophy, following any one of these paths, covers the whole range of immediate experience, the unity of the distinct modes of the Encompassing becomes clear in their interplay and counterplay, in their inseparability, and in their meeting in abstract consciousness. As a totality, this unity is called man, or reason; or, when we give a name to that which we may encounter in immediate experience, it is called Being, God, or the All-Encompassing.

One feature all these philosophical explorations have in common: they try to give a scientific form to something that cannot be an object of science. They speak of something that is the ground of all objectivity, but that is not itself an object. Therefore, Kant called them "transcendental." They do not transcend in a forward direction, so to speak, away from all objects toward something that lies beyond, but in a backward direction, away from all consciousness of objects, toward the ground of possibility of this diverse objectiveness. This accounts for the inadequacy of all propositions advanced in such explorations, although such propositions remain meaningful.

We cannot think unless something becomes an object for us. To be conscious means to live in that clarity which is made possible by the split between the I and the object. But it also means to live within the walls constituted by the split between the I and something known to be an object. We attempt to break out of this prison by becoming conscious of this split in our reflection; and then we realize that wherever men live in serious commitment, the wall has been breached. Objectivity is a mode in which the Encompassing that is lost in the mere object becomes clear. The fact that the Encompassing has also a non-objective aspect becomes apparent in the objectifications of the Encompassing; in each of its modes, objectivity has meaning only in relation to the pertinent subjectivity. This objectivity is the tangible presence of the object in the mode of empirical existence, and logical objectivity in the mode of abstract consciousness. In the mode of *Existenz,* the objective aspect of the Encompassing assumes the form of the tangible presence of transcendence in the myth. If we forget that myth is also a code language, a cipher, it loses all reference to transcendence, it becomes mere tangible presence.

Since nothing becomes clear until it has been made an object, it is not objectification that merits reproach, but only false objectification. Thus, when transcendence is the object of thought in speculation about Being, this object is present in such a way that only its disintegration through the movement of thought shows what was meant. In that way what has been conceived as object is transformed into a sign of possible *Existenz;* when treated as objective *Existentialia* such signs lose their authentic meaning. The question is always how we grasp the indispensable objectivity of things without losing sight of the fact that objectivity alone is insufficient, and how we distinguish it from false objectification.

Now, these are laborious philosophical investigations, worthy of extensive elaboration. It is as someone whose philosophizing has been clarified by such investigations that I shall venture the following remarks on Bultmann's theses.

2. *Myth and Science*

Bultmann, in keeping with a tradition that goes back to Aristotle, distinguishes between myth and science. He regards mythological thinking as obsolete, as something scientific thinking has left behind. However, in so far as the myth conceals a content that was expressed in a language suitable only to the age in which it was created, it must be translated. The myth, says Bultmann, is to be interpreted, divested of its mythological garb, and transposed into a truth valid today.

I deny this. Mythical thinking is not a thing of the past, but characterizes man in any epoch. It is true that the term "myth" is by no means unequivocal. It contains the following elements:

(1) The myth tells a story and expresses intuitive insights, rather than universal concepts. The myth is historical, both in the form of its thinking and in its content. It is not a cloak or disguise put over a general idea, which can be better and more directly grasped intellectually. It explains in terms of historical

origin rather than in terms of a necessity conceived as universal law.

(2) The myth deals with sacred stories and visions, with stories about gods rather than with empirical realities.

(3) The myth is a carrier of meanings which can be expressed only in the language of myth. The mythical figures are symbols which, by their very nature, are untranslatable into other language. They are accessible only in the mythical element, they are irreplaceable, unique. They cannot be interpreted rationally; they are interpreted only by new myths, by being transformed. Myths interpret each other.

How wretched, how lacking in expressiveness our life would be, if the language of myth were no longer valid! To fill mythical forms with banal content is to commit an unpardonable error. The splendor and wonder of the mythical vision is to be purified, but must not be abolished. To speak of "demythologization" is almost blasphemous. Such a depreciation of myth is not enlightenment, but sham enlightenment. Does the splendor of the sunrise cease to be a tangible, ever new and inspiring reality, a mythical presence, just because we know that the earth is revolving around the sun, so that properly speaking there is no sunrise? Does the appearance of the godhead on Mount Sinai or in the burning bush cease to be a poignant reality even when we know that in terms of space and time the phenomena in question were human experiences? To demythologize would be to do away with an essential faculty of our reason. Nevertheless, the impulse to demythologize contains a half-truth derived from genuine enlightenment:

A. *The Degradation of the Myth.* The truth of mythical thinking has been perverted in all periods, including our own: the myth is interpreted not as a code, but literally, and material reality is ascribed to its symbols. Contact with true reality by way of its unique language slips into the materialism of tangibility and usability. Therefore, thinkers of all ages, and Bultmann too, are right in denying assertions which give myth the tangible reality of things in the world, a reality that is accessible to our quite different real knowledge, a knowledge that modern science has developed and clearly delimited. A corpse cannot come to life and rise from the grave. Stories based on the reports of contradictory witnesses and containing scanty data cannot be regarded as historical facts. Because materialism is a common way of thinking, the cipher language of myth will always be degraded into a language of the tangible, which is guaranteed and provides guarantees; this took place among the earliest Christians, and has taken place everywhere in the world. Every epoch has the critical task of correcting such perversions. Bultmann hits on something true in so far as he means by "demythologization" the fulfillment of this task—that of denouncing reification, or conceiving the myth as an alleged reality, opaque and tangible.

B. *Recovery of the Myth.* But the demand for demythologization is justified only if at the same time it insists on restoring the reality of the mythical language. We should seek not to destroy, but to restore the language of myth. For it is the language of a reality that is not empirical, but existential, whereas our mere empirical existence tends continually to be lost in the empirical, as though the latter were all of reality. Only he has the right to demythologize, who resolutely retains the reality contained in the cipher language of the myth.

The real task, therefore, is not to demythologize, but to recover mythical thought in its original purity, and to appropriate, in this form of thinking, the marvelous mythical contents that deepen us morally, enlarge us as human beings, and indirectly bring us closer to the lofty, imageless transcendence, the idea of God which no myth can fully express for it surpasses them all.

Mythical thinking can achieve a unique and legitimate effectiveness in our lives provided that two critical ideas are not lost sight of.

First: Whereas mythical language is historical, and hence its truth can lay no claim to the universal validity of knowledge, it is precisely by virtue of this quality that it can lend the historical *Existenz* something of the unconditional. The unconditional thus brought to light remains conditioned in expression, historically relative, and objectively uncertain. It is one of the basic insights of philosophical reflection that universally valid truth is valid only relatively, from the standpoint of abstract consciousness, while it is existentially neutral; and that existential truth, on the contrary, which becomes identified with the thinker so that he lives and dies in it, precisely for that reason must be historical, and cannot achieve universally valid expression. Only he has a right to live in the mythical who does not confuse the unconditionality of historical *Existenz,* which becomes clear to itself in myth, with the universal validity of an assertion, which, being an assertion concerning an empirical reality, is valid for all. Indeed, the reality that has come down to us in the myth would be lost if it were dissolved into general philosophical ideas.

However, it is impossible to foresee where mythical language achieves validity in the moment of unconditional decision. To learn this language, to appropriate the vision it expresses, makes decision possible and prepares us for it. But even that takes place historically. By entrusting ourselves to our own historical origins we are brought closer to the Bible and to antiquity, despite the partly Oriental contents of the former.

Second: All mythical images are ambiguous. This idea is inherent in the Biblical commandment: Thou shalt not make unto thee any graven image. Everything mythical is a language that grows faint before the transcendence of the one godhead. While we see, hear, and think in the language of myth conceived as code, while we cannot become concretely aware of transcendence without a code language, we must at the same time keep in mind that there are no demons, that there is no magic causality, no such thing as sorcery. There nevertheless remains a deeply moving series of images—the three angels visiting Abraham, Moses receiving the tablets of the law, Isaiah seeing in his vision not God himself but only his manifestation, God addressing one man in thunder and another in a gentle breeze, Balaam's she-ass possessed of better vision than her rider, the Resurrected saying, Touch me not, His Ascension, the Descent of the Holy Ghost, and so on to infinity.

Now, the three distinctions—between the tangible presence and the language of cipher, between mythical contents and the transcendent God, and finally between unconditional historicity and relative universal validity—are proper only to the philosophical consciousness. What we thus distinguish may have been one originally, and it becomes one again where it is alive. For the philosophically naïve, tangible presence and cipher language are not distinct. Some pious people conceive of this tangible presence as an empirical reality. True piety, as a matter of course, eliminates the materialistic, magical, and utilitarian misuse of literal interpretation. There is also an impious, materialistic conception of the myth as tangible reality, which no longer regards the myth as a cipher, and which leads to superstition.

c. *Struggle for Existential Possibilities of Faith.* However, the great and most essential task for anyone who enters the field of mythical thinking is to struggle for the true faith within that thinking. One myth confronts another, not in rational discussion, and not necessarily with the aim of destroying it, but in spiritual struggle. This struggle is fought dishonestly if the outward form of the myth is attacked, if its opponent denounces it as a mode of thinking, denying that such a mode of thinking is necessary to his own faith. Such a struggle is fought fairly and illuminates, when it goes back to the original meanings, to the deeper sources.

Depending on the consequences a given myth has for a given individual, he will accept or reject it, realizing how it affects his actions and conduct. But no man can deny in the name of all, what he rejects for himself. He must concede that a myth which he cannot accept may be valid for others. What is in question is existential truth, which is spiritually efficacious only in mythical thinking, but which without the myth would remain beyond our horizon.

We acquire strength when we read the Bible not in a spirit of slavish literalness, but participating in the inner meanings, rejecting or appropriating them. The mythical contents put the reader in certain states, which he experiences as possibilities; he sees their meanings in the various and variously important images that appear to him, and that all point beyond themselves to something no image can express. It is not rational knowledge, but existential clarification in the sphere of the contradictory, mutually exclusive or complementary possibilities of the Bible that gives us the daily strength to go forward or to resist. For us, the Bible is the favorite arena of spiritual contest; another one is provided by the Greek epic poems and tragedies, and still another by the sacred books of Asia.

Translation, explication, and interpretation in terms of universal concepts—methods which have been practiced since antiquity—may help us to appropriate the contents of the Bible in a limited sense; but the clarifying struggle in which the rejected elements are not destroyed, but retained as discarded possibilities, requires that we come to grips with the living contents of the myth.

Now, it seems to me that in this struggle for the truth of certain Biblical contents against other Biblical contents, Bultmann reaches conclusions which I cannot accept. Here lies the crucial point of the debate. Bultmann, who has made important contributions to our historical knowledge of the New Testament, is interested in all of the Bible as a historian; but as a theologian, he appears in an entirely different light, namely, as a man whose interest in the Bible is singularly restricted. He is almost indifferent to the Old Testament. Study of the Synoptic Gospels proves to him that we have little historical knowledge of Jesus, and that many views contained in those books were a common possession of the non-Christian world at the time. But he attaches the highest value to St. Paul and to the Gospel according to St. John. For him the revelation is found not in a historically knowable Jesus, but in a redemptive history which can be discovered in these later texts. The redemptive history conceived by Christ's disciples and apostles is the very meaning of these texts. Here the emphasis lies on the mythical idea of justification by faith alone—an idea which is most alien to our philosophizing. As a believing reader of the New Testament, Bultmann is attracted by the theology expressed in it, but less so, if at all, by the actual teachings of Jesus. The spiritualized Christ of the Gospel according to St. John, though noble and captivating as a fairy tale hero, seems to us far less significant than the living figure of Jesus in the Synoptics. But Bultmann is not concerned with this. He is scarcely troubled by the absurdity of the Gnostic myth in the Gospel of St. John—although he was the first to recognize it clearly as a myth—and he interprets this Gospel as a surmounting of the myth. His interpretation goes into detail, yet he is scarcely troubled by the fact that this Gospel mythically justifies the earliest Christian anti-Semitism, absent from both St. Paul and the Synoptics and indicative of the sort of faith animating the author of this gospel of love. Selection, emphasis, evaluation, and acceptance or rejection of given contents of the Bible can be clarified only if these are discussed in terms of mythical thinking itself, and we can do this (and do it) today as always.

3. *Faith and Comprehension*

Bultmann presented his ideas under the title of "Faith and Comprehension." Comprehension is the theme of almost all of his discussions: exegesis is his special field, and "existentialist" interpretation is his method of comprehension. Faith is presupposed, and its essential character is brought out through the process of comprehension, namely, as faith in the redemptive history, not as faith in the Resurrection of the Body. Bultmann justifies his comprehension of faith by texts, ascribing to St. John's and St. Paul's writings a higher meaning than to the Synoptic Gospels—and he achieves comprehension of the texts by means of his faith. All comprehension is based on such an inevitable hermeneutic circle, but here the process has a special form because of the absolute character of the faith. Now, the concept of "comprehension" is taken for granted by Bultmann; yet he seems to overlook some of its crucial aspects.

Immediate reality combines elements at which we arrive through critical reflection, and elements present as an inseparable whole in a fulfilled life: significant encounters and meaningless happenings; the personal interventions, demands, and assistance given by the Thou, and the impersonal resistance of things which we conquer or which conquer us; dark powers and clear causes; that which is directly perceived, and that which is logically inferred; passing moods and iron necessity. What is implied by such distinctions within immediate reality, we shall discuss here in greater detail with reference to the meaning of comprehension.

A. *Explanation and Comprehension.* We grasp reality either by explaining it or by comprehending it. What we perceive from the outside as the Other pure and simple, we call nature, and we explain it as a process governed by laws. What we perceive from the inside as the other, but a related Other, we call the soul or the spirit or the person, and we comprehend it as a meaningful whole. In actual fact, in so far as empirical investigation is possible, we explain nature, the cosmos, matter, the unconscious life; we comprehend man and the contents of his spiritual history.

B. *Primary and Secondary Comprehension.* In a broader sense, we call "comprehension" every mode of conceiving reality. Whether we think nature, man, the powers, the gods, God, we speak of "comprehension." In this sense, everything is "comprehended"—nature, the self, God, and so on—and comprehension is the mode of awareness of the Being that we are. Being is the actuality and the effective range of this comprehension.

But here another distinction arises. Anything comprehended by anyone anywhere can be comprehended by us a second time, even though we did not actually participate in or witness the thing in question. We can comprehend Caesar without ourselves being Caesar (Simmel), we can comprehend works of art without creating them ourselves, and scientific discoveries without making them ourselves. In this sense, we not only comprehend, but we comprehend what was comprehended (Böckh: The knowing of the known). This latter type of comprehension is practiced in the grand style by philosophy and the historical sciences that philosophy makes possible—the history of myths, of religion, of art, of language, of literature, of politics, of law, and of philosophy.

What in the sciences we call comprehension as opposed to explanation is a secondary comprehension, not the other, the primary comprehension. Primary comprehension is the reality of comprehension itself; it is in possession of itself and of the thing comprehended; with regard to that reality, secondary comprehension is removed into its own weaker reality. Primary comprehension distinguishes between good and bad, true and false, beautiful and ugly; secondary comprehension, or comprehension of the comprehended, confronts its object from a distance without commitment, and distinguishes only between the correct and the incorrect in determining the actual meaning once intended. Primary comprehension passes judgments of value at every moment; secondary comprehension suspends judgments of value to the extent that it is correct (Weber).

c. *Unity and Tension of Both Types of Comprehension.* This seemingly clear distinction, however, is not actually a clear-cut distinction between two spheres, but the expression of a tension, in which the maximal will to clarity in secondary comprehension provisionally attempts a suspension of value judgments, although the source of all insight and comprehension is actually primary comprehension with its value judgments.

We shall try to make clear this difficulty in the case of the history of ideas, conceived as an empirical science. This history depends upon documents, testimonies, works, and languages in space and time, on things that are present to our senses now, and things that we perceive in the past or over a geographical distance; second, it depends on our ability to comprehend. Just as sensory perception in natural science presupposes sensory organs, so comprehension in the historical sciences presupposes, in addition, a certain intuitive ability. At this point, what we have just asserted as fact, namely, that we can comprehend Caesar without ourselves being Caesar, becomes, instead, a question: How is it possible? What is the relation between comprehension of the comprehended, this reality-less comprehension, to the primary, real comprehension? What is the relation between secondary comprehension and appropriation of the comprehended in one's own reality? The fact that the same term is used for both types of comprehension, the primary and the secondary, shows that there is a connection between the two.

Once again we must make a fundamental distinction, in terms of goals.

The seemingly clear distinction between primary and secondary comprehension is transcended in the primary comprehension itself, which always arises out of something previously comprehended. It is of the essence of the spirit to be born out of its own past. Its primary comprehension feeds on what has been comprehended: spirit itself is history, is spirit by virtue of its own tradition. Spirit, when it is primary, is already past its origins. It alway presupposes a previous comprehension (Hegel). This primary comprehension, arising out of a secondary comprehension, transforms and appropriates but does not possess a yardstick for comprehending correctly what was meant in prior comprehension. Or, it sets out to comprehend the author better than he comprehended himself (the phrase is Kant's, but he himself expects his readers to do just that).

Opposed to this is the other mode of comprehension, the will to comprehend only what has been comprehended, to know and correctly determine what was actually meant in past thoughts, beliefs, works of art, and poetry. It does not let itself be diverted from the goal of correct knowledge of past spiritual creations by the idea, dangerous to the historian but meaningful for the theologian, that one should comprehendingly bring out what was implicit in such creations. Rather, it aims at demonstrating empirically, and as far as possible cogently, what was actually meant, and nothing more.

Now, in that which is primarily comprehended, there is truth and falsity, good and evil, beauty and ugliness. In so far as the latecomer sees these things more clearly in his own primary comprehension, he can have a more complete general view of what was once actually meant, and then demonstrate the errors empirically contained in past spiritual realities. But this applies unequivocally and clearly only to scientific knowledge. Elsewhere there is no general view based on greater knowledge and susceptible of producing better judgment. Rather, the uniqueness of the primary comprehension, which speaks to us out of the past is, by its very nature, inexhaustible. Wherever this is not the case the past spiritual content presents no real interest, no more than past scientific views whose falsity has been demonstrated. The subsequent, secondary, comprehension, where it is confronted with an irreducible primary content, must come to grips with the past, without having an absolute yardstick at its disposal. This coming to grips is only suspended, by no means dispensed with when the historical reality is studied for the purposes of an empirical comprehension.

In other words, this pure, self-effacing secondary comprehension is not a process of passive reproduction. It rests upon one's own latent primary comprehension, now merely suspended. Hence capacity to comprehend in the historical sciences is individually limited, and cannot be uniformly presupposed in all, as we presuppose the presence of sensory organs in all normal persons. For this reason, the achievements of the historical sciences are less cogent, seem less universally valid than those of natural science and are to a far greater degree stamped with personal character.

The capacity for secondary comprehension implies the possibility of being that which is comprehended; it is itself set in motion by this possibility, and is thus participation in some measure. This is true of political insight in the man who has been prevented from political activity; it is true of artistic insight in the man who can grasp art but not create it, who has the capacity for vision but not that for creating aesthetic ideas; it is true of the religious insight of a man who may long for faith but cannot achieve faith, or is prevented from doing so by the self assertion of his reason.

This tension between primary and secondary comprehension has important consequences. There is a wide gap between the man who is himself originally in the act of comprehension, and the man who merely comprehends what the other comprehended.

The comprehending observer may range farther, may gain greater insight than the active participant. But breadth of insight is his at the price of bloodlessness and, moreover, a fundamental limitation: in every case, important elements must elude the mere observer's insight, for the very reason that he is not himself what he comprehends. And our emotional absorption in the experience of secondary comprehension easily leads us into the error of mistaking that comprehension for our own reality. Habituated to such behavior, we fall victim to an illusion: we imagine that comprehension of other people's possibilities can replace our own authentic *Existenz*. For example, we may mistake an uncommitted, aesthetic way of life for our own reality.

D. *Contact with the Incomprehensible.* Primary comprehension comes always into contact with the incomprehensible, which assumes two forms: the incomprehensible which is the obscure pure and simple, and is a natural process capable of explanation; and the incomprehensible which is real in every life, which is also obscure, but which is capable of endless comprehending clarification.

These two types of the incomprehensible correspond to the two methods we have mentioned above: the external, scientific method of explaining the origin of reality in the absolute, unclarifiable obscurity of the Other pure and simple; and that of comprehension, which unfolds meanings and thereby gains insight into historical uniqueness.

The two paths are endless: that of explanation leads to knowledge of the laws governing the processes of nature, which never discloses its inwardness, and which has no inwardness for this type of knowledge; that of comprehension leads to knowledge of meaningful wholes, which always point to deeper meanings. As knowledge advances, we realize ever more unmistakably that in the former case we are coming to grips with an absolute obscurity, with contingent facticity (*Sosein*); in the latter case, with a potential clarity, with something that is fundamentally striving for complete openness.

Each of these cognitive methods leads to a radically different result, but in the transcending thinking of metaphysics, the two may coincide. This is suggested by the fact that human *Existenz* at the profoundest level of awareness seems to unify that which is naturally given and universally explorable with that which is historically comprehensible *ad infinitum* in its uniqueness. For *Existenz* shares in the ambivalence of the incomprehensible itself, which is revealed to the deepest comprehension both as obscurity and as potential clarity.

Comprehension at its best always come to grips with both aspects of the incomprehensible. In contact with the incomprehensible, secondary comprehension becomes primary comprehension: it comes to grips with reality, as a factor of our own historical realization.

E. *Criticism of Bultmann.* Seen in the light of the foregoing distinctions, Bultmann's discussion of comprehension would seem to justify the following conclusions. Because Bultmann, while undoubtedly aware of the difference between primary and secondary comprehension, does not take it into account, the great tension between the two is absent from his writings. He alternates between empirical, philological exegesis and a theological appropriation of religion. The two great opposing goals, which are the historical investigation of religion and the primary comprehension of faith, do not add up to a convincing statement, but rather collapse for lack of tension and clarity. Instead of producing a work that moves us by its inner struggle, Bultmann attempts to be true both to history and to theology, thus keeping his argument at an inferior level. We begin to feel this, when we recall our situation with regard to the incomprehensible.

When we have run headlong into the wall of the incomprehensible, are we still within the range of comprehension? Is clarification still possible at this point? Only in one sense was the incomprehensible a fundamental limit: the more our knowledge of nature advances, the greater and the more unsurmountable the obscurity of the ultimate incomprehensible. We encounter this limit even in the realm of the spirit in so far as it is tied to nature, for instance, when we are deaf to argument, inaccessible to rational persuasion, when comprehension breaks off, or when the incomprehensible asserts itself concealed within the superficially comprehensible. But in the other sense, the incomprehensible confronts us with the possibility of an infinite progression in comprehension, with the striving of rational *Existenz* to disclose itself.

When the will to comprehend (which does not content itself with external cognition) runs headlong into the incomprehensible, the latter either shows itself in mythical figures and speculative concepts, as though it were striving to disclose itself, but still concealed in magnificently ambiguous language—or the incomprehensible becomes accessible to endless existential communication between men.

Faith sees the two aspects of the incomprehensible as one, by a primary comprehension, first in mythical, then in conceptual terms, without really comprehending it. Faith runs headlong into the incomprehensible and makes us aware of it in those terms. This faith can be communicated to others, and thereby lays claim to being comprehended. Only what can be comprehended can be communicated.

Therefore, when Bultmann combines faith with comprehension, he goes to the heart of the matter. A question, however, remains: how is comprehension effected when it comes up against the incomprehensible? "Existentialist" interpretation scarcely provides scientific insight; its objectifications are false. Even when this objectification is consciously rejected, its effects linger, though they may be unnoticed. The result is a false knowledge, and a faith inauthentic in its modes of communication. On the other hand, it is true that comprehension of faith, when it has weight, is "existential" interpretation in terms of communication. Such comprehension has nothing to do with scientific method; it is a voice from the source. We cannot achieve such comprehension in the noncommittal spirit of scientific cognition, for there is no scientific cognition here. We can achieve it only in the spirit of responsible commitment and acceptance. In these matters, to comprehend is to circle around, to describe, to discuss, to transform. To speak from faith is itself faith, preparation for the existential moment, recall to the eternal ground in the language of mythical images—or, in philosophy, in the language of speculative concepts.

All of us live in images, even if we go beyond them in philosophical speculation. We might think of them as constituting an unavoidable myth—a myth that may be shallow or profound, that may inspire a madness concealing boredom, that may gratify, for one destructive moment, a craving for the monstrous, or that may lead to the most extraordinary self-sacrifice in failure. Philosophically speaking, the myth is the rational a priori form in which we become aware of transcendence. Psychologically speaking, it is the mode of experiencing the real. But neither rational a priori form nor psychological experiential form is a guarantee of truth. Either of these forms may serve as vehicle for the hysteria of every sort of magician or Pied Piper, every sort of opportunist who believes and yet does not believe, who lies and is taken in by his own lies, who dazzles and spellbinds his victims, whether in the guise of the aesthetic snob or that of the nihilistic politician. All of them are destructive, whether of self-knowledge and possible authenticity, or of life itself.

The truth of the myth is not inherent in the a priori form or in the psychological disposition. Only moral earnestness can arouse moral earnestness. The man who speaks in mythical language has assumed a real risk. He has taken upon his conscience to identify himself with his works, not just for the moment, but forever.

Bultmann speaks neither as the nihilistic spellbinder nor as the authentic man of faith. He speaks as a scientist, and his intentions are of the best. But because he advances theological propositions in the name of "abstract scientific consciousness," steeped as he is in false notions of modern science and misled by his belief in an allegedly scientific philosophy, his words lack palpable conviction. Theological propositions, just like philosophical ones, lose all meaning when they hide behind science, i.e., when the pneuma does not inform them. It is for just this reason that theology grounds its comprehension in the Holy Ghost. No one can, of course, be sure whether the spirit bloweth or bloweth not at a given time and place; but he to whom the spirit speaks, however faintly, must say when he was moved by it, and when he was not. He should also be able to describe the silence of the spirit. When the mythical contents are genuinely appropriated, the speaker communicates his conviction out of the faith in whose name he speaks; he is not then troubled by the inherent implausibility of the myth in its literal aspect. Now, Bultmann, we feel, assumes scientific responsibility for his statements, a responsibility which is fully adequate in historical investigation, but which is insufficient when theological questions are at stake. The true man of faith speaks out of the Encompassing, in which the objectivity of what is said and the subjectivity of the speaker are not separated. But when the subjective aspect is neglected in favor of the mere objectivity of the content of faith or of the objectified subjectivity of existentialist thinking, the genuine theological or philosophical commitment—a commitment which is impossible in science—is lost; serious commitment is also lost when the objective aspect is sacrificed in favor of an arbitrary or fanatic subjectivity. Bultmann seems to mistake exegesis for compre-

hension of faith. It is as though he had thrown overboard th
broad range of possibilities, the tensions and decisions, which ar
inseparable from genuine comprehension.

III. THE FORCES BEHIND THE DISCUSSION: TRANSFORMATION AND APPROPRIATION OF BIBLICAL RELIGION

To sum up: The transcendental analyses that branch out int
the methodology of comprehension and exegesis are ambivalen
in character. On the one hand, they open up and divide the area
of our knowledge, of our consciousness of reality, of our self
understanding. They are critical, i.e., they guard against con
fusion. By going back to the original sources, they enable us t
preserve meaningful contents that have falsely been declare
invalid. They strive to be critically neutral, not to prejudge any
thing regarding the contents of myth. They clarify the groun
on which meanings expressible in words can confront each other
They keep open the possibilities for awareness of the real.

On the other hand, such discussions always serve as a curtair
behind which something else takes place, something that reall
matters: in our case, the issue is the appropriation of the Biblica
faith and its transformation into a faith effective today. Wher
we step behind the curtain, the questions at once take on anothe
complexion. What so far has been touched upon casually, now
becomes the theme.

A genuine transformation of living religion cannot be effecte
by deliberate planning. Such a transformation must be actuall
under way before one can speak in its name. The critique of
theology will then raise the crucial question—a question tha
cannot be expressed in scientific terms—namely, whether thi
transformation has any meaning for contemporary believers, anc
what this meaning may be.

Theologians sometimes dodge the existential claim by speaking about it, by acquiring an intellectual knowledge of faith, and by working for the preservation of the church: of course, the tendency to self-perpetuation is inherent in every human institution. Theology may also serve an entirely different purpose—that of ingeniously remolding a religion which is no longer believed, but is still desired, into a form acceptable to "the educated among the scornful," while passing over in silence the vital issues. Such a theology may be motivated by social considerations and by whatever still remains of the traditional beliefs.

How do we relate Bultmann to such ideas? Once again, we must first define the horizon within which an answer is possible. We shall discuss three points. First, the minister in his community; second, the struggle between liberalism and orthodoxy at the level of faith; third, the unification of theology and philosophy, both as aspiration and as threat.

1. *The Ministry*

Biblical faith is not acquired by study, but by the practice of religion. The language of faith is not acquired by translating the myths into supposedly nonmythological terms, but by transforming the content of the myth itself, by giving it meanings cogent in our own time.

Bultmann seems to solve this problem by criticism and the elimination of the scientifically untenable, as though the mere negative effect of such a purge sufficed to bring about a rebirth, as though mythical language should be discarded as such. Because Bultmann fails to recognize that the mythical language conveys an untranslatable truth, his thinking does not strike us as inspiring. In my opinion, it is poor, and even stultifying. The element of truth in the myth, which persists throughout its transformations, cannot be separated from its historical garb, once the latter has been stripped away. Exegesis, let alone existentialist interpretation, cannot supply anyone with a "knowledge" of the Biblical faith.

Generally speaking, the task of acquiring faith is only secondarily a question of theological scholarship; primarily it is a matter of the minister's own theology in his daily practice, as he comes to grip with specific human situations and proves his worth. Nor is it a task for philosophy, even though philosophy may formally illuminate the approaches to the transcendent, may clarify the transcendent at the existential level, and may help to decipher the cipher language of the transcendent.

The practical minister (and today the cure of souls is widely practiced—in a highly questionable manner—outside the churches, in the fields of psychotherapy, anthroposophy, Christian Science, etc.) is confronted with an extraordinary task. He boldly sets out to understand the language of transcendence (which he conceives as the language of God) and to speak it himself in his community, commenting on men and events, human aspirations and failures. Only a man who is himself permeated with such language has the right to use it. It is authentic when spoken by a man who actually participates; it is inauthentic in a man who merely thinks it, or, worse yet, merely uses the words. Where it is authentic, and hence efficacious—as at the deathbed, at weddings, burials, in times of adversity—it serves its purpose. At such times it gives us a sense of our own finiteness, helps us to arrive at certainty. The minister who thus proves himself can do things unattainable by philosophizing: he can perform the communal rites and administer the sacraments, and celebrate the holy feasts in holiness.

The priest who performs the sacred rites, the pastor who preaches the revelation, the theologian who knows the secrets of divinity, together constitute a primal human phenomenon, which, under a variety of names, is always manifesting itself anew. When we realize the tremendous responsibilities implied in such a calling, we are filled with admiration and concern. This is indeed a bold venture, to seek salvation through one's own life and in one's own commitment, not merely for the self, but for all. The minister's action is not confined to sympathy and aid; it also commands belief through his personality. Even when he struggles unremittingly, even though he has no direct knowledge of salvation, he stands already in the truth. In him the mythical language acquires efficacy. He makes the mythical world his own, and gives it present meaning, not with the help of the theories of philosophers and theologians, but by the genuineness and the depth of his own experience of faith.

The implications of all this will perhaps be clearer if we recall what may bar the way to the religious vocation. This calling is impossible for all who are susceptible of disappointment in the majority, of disillusionment with the human community, its lack of understanding or honesty. A man for whom faith has become absolute inwardness, to whom all that is temporal has become unimportant, who regards all material objects of worship as external and hence to be repudiated—such a man cannot be a priest or a pastor. The religious calling is incompatible with a view that radically negates the world as total evil, with the belief that the world is at an end, is lost, that there remains only contemplation in despair. Men like Sebastian Franck or Kierkegaard, who possessed such characteristics, attempted in vain to be or to become ministers.

There is perhaps a certain analogy between the callings of the minister and the physician. In both cases, the practical aspect of the work takes precedence over theoretical knowledge, which is only an auxiliary. The future of the physician's art is not determined in the laboratories devoted to medical research, nor is the future of the Biblical faith decided by academic theology.

Intellectual refinements have little bearing on practical achievements in these fields. Kierkegaard's conception of the Christian faith as absurd is admirably consistent and seductive. If this conception were true, it would, as it seems to me, spell the end of the Biblical religion. Without comparing it to Bultmann's more anodyne conception, we may observe that Bultmann's radical purge of religion in favor of a redemptive process implies belief in another absurdity, which, however, avoids Kierkegaard's consequences. In each case, a doctrine intended to counteract a false rationalism unwittingly provides the unbeliever with a means to persevere in his faith with good conscience, at the price of violence to his reason.

Today the crucial practical elements of the physician's art and of Biblical religion are passed over in silence, while medical research and theological speculations are loudly publicized. Thus, a kind of acoustic illusion is produced, which misleads as to the true state of affairs.

The analogy between modern man's attitude to the pastor and to the physician may be illustrated by Bultmann's statement that "in cases of illness, we cannot . . . resort to medical and clinical remedies and at the same time believe in the New Testament's spirits and miracles." The fact is, we can do this very well. There is worse: modern superstitious belief in medicine is frequently just as absurd as the literal belief in spirits and miracles. And physicians infected by the psychoanalytic religion or by similar contemporary movements descend into demonology, although they express themselves in a somewhat different language.

Bultmann wastes his critical energies on denouncing relatively insignificant dangers. But against the real dangers that threaten us today, against the deceptive hopes and expectations derived from fear and conceived in helplessness and confusion, against the facile expedients resorted to by medicine, politics, and theology with uniformly ruinous effects, Bultmann provides no remedy. He does not take part in the struggle against them. He confines himself to theoretical discussion, which combines shallow enlightenment with religious orthodoxy, a discussion which, for all its differences, is essentially carried on in the spirit of the rationalistic theology that Lessing once repudiated in favor of either genuine orthodoxy or genuine liberalism. We shall discuss this point at greater length.

2. *Orthodoxy and Liberalism*

What is actually hidden in the debate on demythologization is the struggle of orthodoxy against liberalism. Where does Bultmann stand in this struggle? Before answering this question, we must agree on the meanings of the terms "orthodoxy" and "liberalism."

A. *The Liberal Faith.* Liberalism is not based on abstract, intellectual understanding or on unhistorical criticism. The liberal thinker knows that philosophical justifications of religion, as well as theological speculations, serve no purpose if the main thing is lacking, namely, faith. And what matters is not the verbal expression of religious ideas, not creeds, but men living in a community of faith. This community is rooted in a historical tradition whose authority is respected, but is nevertheless subject to change.

In other words: Liberalism recognizes the validity of both the objective and the subjective aspect of faith, and regards the two aspects as inseparable. Liberal faith is characterized by its conception of the objective aspect. The features of physical presence and knowledge are pushed into the background without being completely eliminated. The language of liberalism is less positive than that of orthodoxy. Liberalism furthers faith, not by credos, but in the actual conduct of life. It gives up all superstition, i.e., all absolutization of the object. It preserves, within knowledge, an area of nonknowledge, which comprises the symbols of transcendence. It recognizes the physical aspects of faith as such symbols, not as actual presences of transcendence in the world.

The liberal faith is self-sustained, drawing its strength directly from transcendence, seeking no guarantee in the sensory world or in tradition, though the tradition awakens it and makes it capable of testing the traditional truths. The liberal faith needs no external props, not even a redemptive history conceived as an objective absolute event, the prerequisite of all faith.

In liberalism everything is centered on the responsibility of man thrown back upon himself. It is through freedom, and only through freedom, that he experiences how he is given to himself by transcendence in freedom—not by freedom.

B. *Orthodox and Liberal Attitudes Toward the Incomprehensible.* We have previously referred to the limits of comprehension. Everywhere we run headlong into the incomprehensible. We encounter it as a wall, as silent nature which does not answer our questions, either when we master it or when it resists our efforts or even destroys us. We also encounter the incomprehensible in men who cannot be moved, who speak but do not answer, and in our ownselves, where it often makes us act against our will, and pretends to be ourselves.

Our comprehension is a movement in an area that is surrounded by the incomprehensible on all sides—a movement which on the one hand confronts the incomprehensible pure and simple and recognizes it ever more clearly as the dark ground of the natural process governed by laws. On the other hand, this movement experiences the incomprehensible as something that can be clarified endlessly, as something that is not fundamentally and absolutely incomprehensible, but rather striving to be comprehended.

Orthodoxy and liberalism are characterized by their attitude toward this movement of progressing comprehension. Where the progress is arrested, we have orthodoxy; where it goes on, we have liberalism. Everything ready-made, every kind of self-sufficient dogmatic knowledge is illiberalism. Illiberalism can be discovered in every man at the point where he no longer listens or gives answers, or where he answers inadequately; we discover this temptation in ourselves. To know this, to try to detect illiberalism in ourselves, to recognize that our opponents help us in this self-testing and to welcome them for that reason, are fundamental traits of the liberal attitude.

c. *Liberalism and Enlightenment.* Liberalism is in alliance with enlightenment, but the genuine kind of enlightenment—the irresistible, responsible movement of reason, which is never completed. Sham enlightenment, on the other hand, is rational knowledge taken as complete.

The sham kind of enlightenment exists in all historical periods. It is, in effect, a form of unfaith which superstitiously believes itself to be firmly grounded in rationality. It is seduced by cogent insights, which are in contradiction to falsely understood, or even perverted, statements of religious faith. It has a certain power in so far as it is based on such insights.

This is why theologians attempt repeatedly to defend faith against enlightenment by accepting the unavoidable insights with which enlightenment threatens to destroy faith. They hope to defeat the adversary by seizing his own weapons. In this battle, Bultmann applies a familiar strategy: he appropriates a maximum of enlightenment, only in order to assert faith all the more resolutely. But it seems to me that he appropriates an enlightenment that is not genuine, and a scientific philosophy that is not scientific—in the end to assert an absurd dogma and cling to it at all costs, with a determination that smacks of violence. As a result, we are once again confronted with the defects that characterize all such enterprises: they fail to satisfy the unbeliever, and implant doubts in the believer. From the liberal point of view, Bultmann offers a deceptive solution, in order to bolster orthodoxy with the help of the method of existentialist interpretation.

Liberalism, which is inspired by genuine enlightenment, by the unending movement of reason, emancipates itself from all scientific superstition, from all allegedly scientific philosophy, as well as from orthodoxy. It does not try to defend religion. Lessing, the prototype of the liberal, and one of liberalism's greatest manifestations, turned against the violent kind of orthodoxy, against the enlightened rationalistic theology that wanted to defend or conserve religion by reinterpreting its teachings, as well as against the destructive ideas of Reimarus, so complacent in his rationalism. Lessing stood aloof from such as these, never imagining that he saw the whole truth. With his endless critical energy he remained open to the contents of the Bible. He condemned half-truths, obscurity, self-delusion. Therefore, without being an orthodox believer himself, he favored straightforward, devout orthodoxy in its naïve form (without, however, approving the dishonest intolerance of a Pastor Götze). He respected Reimarus' arguments as important for getting at the truth, but he recognized their limits and where he went beyond them. Least of all did he favor the rationalism of the theologians, who, inconsistent and irresolute, wanted to conserve religion, but, for all their good intentions, became untruthful. In Bultmann I find nothing of a Lessing, a Kant, a Goethe, none of the liberal spirit, but something of their opponents. Occasionally he seems to be giving a new form to the old theological rationalism; at other times, to be re-founding orthodoxy.

D. *Ambiguity of the Terms, Enlightenment, Liberalism, Conservatism.* Enlightenment, liberalism, conservatism are ambiguous terms. They are confusing unless one distinguishes between enlightenment as progressive emancipation from one's self-caused immaturity (Kant), and enlightenment as know-it-allness (sham

enlightenment); between liberalism as limitless openness to reason—i.e., communication for the purpose of furthering all genuine insights, however opposed to each other—and liberalism as
the intolerant absolutizing of an allegedly definitive intellectual
knowledge of the freedom and equality of all men, which would
in effect justify all arbitrary impulses; and between conservatism
as reverence for tradition and resistance to wanton destruction of
the past, and conservatism as hostility to progress, as an attempt
to freeze human institutions and ideas.

Genuine enlightenment, liberalism, and conservatism form a
harmonious whole, and are opposed to the powers of sham rationalism, false liberalism, and reaction, which, though often in conflict with one another, are related in spirit.

E. *The Idea of Revelation.*   Liberal faith is distinguished from
orthodoxy by its attitude toward the idea of revelation. The belief
that God manifests himself at a given place and time, that He
has revealed himself directly at one place and time and only there
and then, makes God appear as a fixed thing, an object in the
world. This objective entity is supposed not only to be revered on
the basis of tradition, but also to possess the absoluteness of godhead. In the canonic writings, in the creed and in the system of
dogmas, in the sacrament of Holy Orders, in the church as *corpus
mysticum Christi,* and in other forms, the revelation and the
grace it bestows are conceived as physically present.

Liberal faith rejects this conception of revelation. It recognizes
that the revelation of truth is a mystery, a series of sudden illuminations in the history of the mind; it recognizes that we are igno-
rant of how men arrived at this revelation, and that some of its
elements have not yet been comprehended. The fact that we use
the same term, "revelation," to denote both an absolute and
unique divine intervention and this process of the gradual revelation of truth, must not cause us to overlook the radical difference between the two.

The liberal faith is criticized by orthodoxy on the ground that it makes man the master, who by his own thought determines what God can and should do, and what God can say. On this basis liberalism is identified with disbelief, and it is argued that instead of doing all the talking, man should let God speak to him. According to the Bible, man is capable of knowledge only in so far as he is known by God. Hence, the great alternative is ultimately formulated in these terms: Is man with his reason master and judge of everything that is, can be, and should be, or must he listen to God? (Fries, in *Tübinger Theologische Quartalschrift,* 1952, p. 287.) Orthodoxy demands profession of faith in revelation—for instance in "the gospel of Crucifixion and Resurrection" —and asserts that what is at stake in our attitude toward this gospel is "the decision between faith and unfaith, and in this decision, the issue is between eternal life and eternal death" (*Denkschrift der Tübinger Fakultät,* p. 34). The reply to this, from the standpoint of liberal faith is:

(1) How do we recognize revelation? What criterion of truth is given for the direct revelation of God? The point at issue here is that, according to orthodoxy, the revelation is its own criterion. But in actual fact, whatever is said and done in the name of revelation, is said and done in worldly form, in worldly language, in human acts and human perceptions.

Those who believe in a revealed faith argue that its divine origin guarantees the revelation. Revelation, they maintain, is distinguished from all myth by the exclusiveness, uniqueness, and absoluteness of its demand for faith. This assertion, however, does not change the fact that revelation has all the features of myth. Liberal faith does not deny that God can act as absolute transcendence, but it insists that all it can perceive is the actions, the sayings, and the experiences of human beings.

(2) What is crucial is that God is hidden. Whatever is posited as an absolute in the world, as God's word or God's act, is in each

case a human act or human word that demands that we recognize it as God's. However, the idea of the hidden God can be interpreted mythically in rational terms, as Kant did. According to Kant, God manifests His eternal wisdom by remaining hidden. For if God Himself in all his majesty appeared before us or spoke to us, he says, we would be reduced to the status of marionettes, unable to move save when our strings were pulled. But God willed that we should find our way to Him by means of our freedom; and this way leads to Him, because our self-responsible reason in the world perceives His ambiguous hints, and arrives at Him through the reality of our moral life.

Liberal faith refuses to arrest its movement in time by a revelation frozen in its definitiveness. It strives to keep itself open, ready to recognize the language of the godhead in everything that is real. It perceives the hidden God's demand upon us, a demand inherent in the fact that He is hidden. This faith therefore forbids absolute obedience to the words of a sacred text or to the authority of an ecclesiastical official, because (according to it) every man can be in direct relation to the godhead in his freedom and reason, which constitute a higher authority. And this higher authority may require that every revered transition be tested anew and transformed.

Speaking in mythical terms, we may say: liberal faith opposes the assertion of a direct revelation, not out of a will to empty freedom, but out of its idea of God as actualized in mankind's relations with the hidden, all-guiding transcendence.

(3) The orthodox objection against liberalism—that it fails to recognize the objective character of God's actions and that it invests the human subject with supreme authority—is misleading.

The attempt to play objectivity against the subject, like the inverse attempt to play subjectivity against objectivity, is based on failure to recognize the fundamental structure of our empirical existence and consciousness. There can be no object without a subject, and no subject without an object; the Encompassing in which we exist and which we are, is clarified through the inter-action between the two; it eludes us if we confine ourselves either to subject without object, or to object without subject. Empirical existence implies an environment, abstract consciousness implies objectivity, and *Existenz* implies transcendence.

Transcendence, God, the All-Encompassing never become clear to us as they are apart from our subjectivity. The reality of tran-scendence is present for us objectively only in the language of the code or cipher, not as it is in itself. Transcendence is reality only for *Existenz*. Both transcendence and *Existenz* manifest themselves in empirical existence and in consciousness, but only as languages. God's countenance, God's action, God's word—all these are only code symbols by means of which a subject with potential *Existenz* conceives, perceives, and questions that which is manifested to it as a reality.

It is not true that the liberal believer presumes to decide what is and what is not possible for God. But as a philosopher he is aware that objective knowledge is subject to conditions rooted in the structure of Being as it is given to us.

As we have said, the Encompassing is clarified within the split between subject and object. This does not mean, however, that we determine that which our thinking discloses as the Other. We are moved by the Other, and we conceive it as independent of us, as something that is even without us. At the same time, we be-come aware of the subjective conditions governing our aware-ness of everything objective. Reality is disclosed to us only in so far as we are empirically existent, as knowable only in so far as we are abstract consciousness; and as transcendence only in so far as we are potential *Existenz*. The unfolding of subjectiv-ity implies the coming into view of a pertinent objectivity. The one does not produce the other, but the object appears only to the subject, and the subject can realize itself only through the object.

From the standpoint of liberal philosophy, the thesis that the revelation of God is an event taking place in the world is based on a confusion. For it is a fallacy to say that transcendence is the object of *Existenz* conceived as subject, and that the one is related to the other as the known is related to knowledge in the world. The transcendence that does not speak ambiguously in the language of code but is there unambiguously in the revelation, is, after all merely the Bible, the church, merely an assertion by men who claim to have seen God, to have heard His voice, to have witnessed His acts. They demand belief in their assertions, and call this belief faith. Thus, a worldly authority, which in every instance has a human and historical foundation, lays claim to have its source in God.

Now, we may ask: Does the revelation as an objective reality come first, and does faith follow from the perception of its reality? Or is faith in the revelation at one with, and inseparable from, the revelation itself, which produces the faith? As in all our awareness, here the subject is bound to the object, and the object to the subject. Is revelation that which always takes place when there is faith, when God is believed in? Have such revelations occurred whenever they have been asserted in history, not only in the West (Judaism, the various Christian denominations, Islam), but also in Asia?

Or do we go counter to the meaning of revelation when we assert that it is a general phenomenon, of which the revelations of Jesus Christ or of Moses are only special cases? Are the other cases—of the eternal Vedas to the Rishis, or of the canonic books to the Chinese—not cases of revelation? Can the claim of a revelation to uniqueness be justified, or is it inherently unjustified?

Or, are we to conceive of revelation so broadly that every man in his freedom has the possibility of experiencing himself as being given and guided by transcendence, despite the ambiguity of all the worldly signs?

Such questions can be answered when we keep in mind that the subject and the object are inseparable in the Encompassing, which is clarified by their division. Hence, the answers logically take the form of a circle. We say either that revelation is the process of becoming revealed to the subject, which conceives revelation in itself as something objective; or, that reason in the movement of reason subjects its revelation to the test of rationality. We have here the circle of subject and object which, in various ways, condition, justify, and support each other. Inescapably, the circle is the fundamental form of all our awareness. The discovery that an idea implies a circle does not necessarily prove the falsity of this idea. What matters, rather, is to ascertain the depth or shallowness, the adequacy or inadequacy of a given circle, the consequences of thinking or living in a given circle. We do not emerge from such circles, even when we surmount each separate circle. Nor can we, from a purely logical point of view, prefer one of the circles to another. For instance, materialism, too, implies a circular reasoning: the world is a product of our brain; the brain is a product of the world; and through the brain the world perceives itself in this product. The circle of reason in liberal faith, and the circle of the revealed faith in orthodoxy, are in conflict not because either has a right to reject the other on the ground that it involves a circular reasoning, but only on the basis of the content and consequences of each.

(4) Liberalism recognizes the historical sources of our spiritual life, whatever they may be. For instance, we Westerners recognize the importance of the Bible. But liberalism repudiates the idea of an exclusive truth formulated in a credo. It recognizes that the way to God is possible also without Christ, and that the Asians can find it without the Bible.

Liberalism understands the importance of history and its language for faith. The main thing for liberalism is to see to it that faith is not weakened by the denial that historical objectification is absolutely and universally valid, i.e., by the denial that faith can find objective guarantees in the world. Philosophical reflection (e.g., Kant's transcendental philosophy and its successors) is a necessity for liberal faith, and can be helpful, not because it can provide us with contents of faith, but because it opens our minds to faith by clearing the ground and enabling us to become aware of the truth inherent in faith, as contrasted with unfaith and with orthodoxy.

Every tradition is valid as a possible language, and becomes a true language not abstractly, but in given historical situations for *Existenz,* which discovers itself in them. The historical struggle at the existential level takes place in the medium of the mythical. Rational and mythical modes of awareness are only the foreground of a never-ending process of existential clarification and comprehension.

(5) While liberalism repudiates an objective redemptive history conceived as an absolute event and as a prerequisite of salvation for all men, it accepts this history as a myth. As in the case of other myths, the validity of this one must be tested existentially, and judged on the basis of the strength that emanates from its language, the truth that arises from it in the reality of life. Liberalism recognizes faith in revelation, including belief in the truth of the redemptive history as a possible truth valid for him who believes it—in so far as the believer does not, by his deeds or his words, draw consequences destructive to the freedom of men who find themselves directly before God, nor attempt to coerce others by violent means.

Considering the kind of theology that is still current today, Buri displayed great courage in drawing the ultimate consequences from Bultmann's demythologization. Buri admits candidly that the redemptive history is no more than a myth. But he does not want to demythologize in order to destroy. While recognizing that the language of religion is mythical through and through, Buri asserts its validity as a language, and tries with its help to gain awareness of our beliefs, moral duties, hopes, and goals. Now it is no longer the creed that guides us, but moral earnestness and serious commitment undertaken in uncertainty, without outside guarantees. Clarification of transcendence is based upon the concrete situation.

(6) The conflict between the claims of orthodoxy and the liberal reaction they provoked was extraordinarily passionate because of the importance of the issue—the decision concerning our eternal salvation. We can still feel faint echoes of this passion today.

For almost two thousand years orthodoxy has threatened us with eternal death, condemning our self-deification, our pride, our presumption in setting man, i.e., ourselves, above God. These judgments fill us with amazement, as do the uncritical, curious assertions that condemn the nonbeliever to eternal torments and promise the believer eternal bliss.

Is God absent from our lives? Is our trust that God comes to our aid in a manner that is for us incomprehensible, unpredictable, and incalculable—that when we act with good will He can be with us in the terrors of destruction and death—a mad delusion? Bultmann says that the idea of God without Christ is to be described as madness "from the point of view of the Christian faith."

Are we not justified in thinking that God would not damn us for our honest efforts even if orthodoxy were right, and even though these efforts continually fail and deceive us? Did not God side with Job against the orthodox theologians?

He who lives by human reason must not, in struggling against others, justify himself by God, but only by worldly arguments. For God is my adversary's God as well as my own. But what if orthodox fanatics deny us the right to serve God, to strive to live in obedience to God, denouncing our idea of God as a delusion? Against intolerance only intolerance is effective, but fortunately this is no longer a matter of life and death. Heretics are no longer burned at the stake in the name of the revelation (although we should never forget that the extermination of heretics is consistent with such beliefs); today they are destroyed in the name of authorities other than God. Fortunately, since the anathemas the orthodox theologians still pass are inconsequential, we may refrain from answering them on this point.

F. *Is Bultmann a Liberal or an Orthodox?*   In the light of the foregoing observations, we may attempt to answer the question, Where does Bultmann stand?

However reliable and many-sided Bultmann may be as a historian, as a theologian he leads us astray. He seems to be saying something but in the end does not; he seems to be saving the faith, but he does not save it. When—and this is crucial—he asserts a frozen orthodoxy of redemption, he undermines it at the same time by the highhandedness of his assertion. His rehashing of the old problems of enlightenment, ostensibly intended to salvage an essential minimum of faith, must delight secret unbelievers among the theologians, because he dispenses them from believing a great number of things; at the same time, he must displease the orthodox believers, because he deprives them of so many of their best arguments.

He has not discovered a new form for the language of faith, although he thinks that his existentialist interpretation provides a new method for the true acquisition of faith. This idea is not only untenable philosophically, in my opinion, but I should also imagine it to be of little practical value to the pastor.

The philosopher cannot help being taken aback when he sees what this salvaged minimum of faith turns out to be—the residue of faith which, according to Bultmann, is not mythical, and is the essential element of religion: namely, justification by faith alone, faith in the redemptive history. For a philosopher this is the most alienating, the most outlandish of beliefs—this Lutheran dogma with its terrible consequences scarcely seems any longer even denotative existentially. Bultmann himself sums up and discloses the meaning of his enterprise in the statement that "Radical demythologization parallels the Pauline-Lutheran doctrine of justification by faith alone without the works of law." It seems to me that Bultmann's position is in effect altogether orthodox and illiberal, despite his liberalism as a man and a historian.

Bultmann's illiberalism may be characterized as follows:

A philosophy that conceives empirical existence as hopeless (and Heidegger's *Sein und Zeit* can be interpreted as such a philosophy) finds its natural complement in a doctrine that promises salvation through faith in the redemptive history. The sinner, who realizes the full extent of his sinfulness only through grace, sees this grace as an objective event which can save him if he believes in it.

But such an analysis of empirical existence is not universally valid. It does not reflect a general human truth, though some, perhaps many, but certainly not all, men recognize themselves in it. The reality of man is not a radical sinfulness which is overcome only by an alleged divine intervention that took place in a foreign country a long time ago.

We find in the Biblical faith itself an entirely different conception of man—namely the conception of man's God-created inborn nobility, *nobilitas ingenita,* as the Pelagians called it. Man, always in danger, is humble in the knowledge that he is not self-created, and that in fulfilling the task assigned to him he must be given to himself in order not to lose himself. According to this conception, man is determined by God, the source of everything man can be, but only in the direct relation of his own freedom to the godhead, and without the help of an external agency. Thus man is confident that he can fulfill the will of the hidden God by an effort entirely subjected to his own responsibility, and that he will be helped by God in an incomprehensible and unpredictable way. This God-given *nobilitas ingenita* is called in Biblical thinking "the Christ in me," and is not a possession, is not ours once and for all, but must be continually conquered, and can be lost. This conception of man, of his freedom, and of his task, is that of liberalism.

3. *The Unification of Theology and Philosophy*

The natural tendency of liberalism—a tendency for which it is criticized, regarded with concern, or viewed with satisfaction— seems to be in the direction of a meeting of philosophy and theology; these might ultimately be united, as they were in Plato, in the Stoics, in Origen, in St. Augustine, and in Nicholas of Cusa. Should this come to pass, we must keep in mind an important distinction: theology and philosophy may become one, but not religion and philosophy. In religion there flows a stream of communal life that lies beyond the reach of philosophy—a living relationship to shrines, to sacred actions, objects, and books, to rites and prayers, to the office of the priest, in short to the physical presence of symbols. Here philosophy ends and is confronted with something that is not philosophy.

Philosophy and all great philosophers stand outside this sacred world. A philosophy that could cross this gulf would not arrive at one particular religion, but at a religion embracing all religions (thus Proclus called himself the hierophant of the whole world): from the religious point of view, a contradiction in terms. It would be the abolition of the historicity of religion, of its historical earnestness. What has been called "philosophical religion" would be a religion without any of the features of a living religion, it would be what was left after all the rituals, the prayers, the religious communities, and the Scriptures had been subtracted. Schelling's philosophy of mythology and the revelation, which aims at such a philosophical religion, ends, it is true, in Christ, and even seems the narrower thereby. But Schelling's positive philosophy of the historicity of the real implies elimination of the Christian idea.

Philosophy should not offer its services to those who seek to formulate a philosophical alternative to religion; rather it should warn against itself.

When theology becomes philosophical to such a point that it loses touch with the specific elements of religion, the philosopher may very well be alarmed. It is as though his indispensable adversary, in struggling against whom he clarifies and rekindles his own impulses, were no longer there. He wonders what form the old adversary, now hidden, has assumed. It is as though he could not do without his adversary, whom he had actually never wanted to destroy, but only to induce to speak with the utmost frankness.

The philosopher is alarmed about the fate of the majority because he is aware of the impotence of philosophizing. A theology that has become identical with philosophy might bog down in the same impotence. Now, the philosopher's right to address himself to individuals is denied to theology, which must address itself to every member of the church. The question is whether the very thing in which philosophy must fail is not indispensable to the majority of us—namely, religion as worship, as community, as tangible and authoritative physical presence. The philosopher may fear lest the things that philosophy cannot do, and that it legitimately expects religion to do—in as much as not everyone remains content with philosophical insight—may now not be done at all.

Furthermore a unification of theology and philosophy may

adversely affect the fate of the Biblical teachings. The Biblical impulses which for us are irreplaceable, may be watered down, as a prelude to their complete disappearance, instead of being remolded and renewed.

Finally, the philosopher today knows that men who have become helpless through their reliance upon mere understanding, and have not attained to philosophy, fall prey to a tyranny which is all the more terrible because it recognizes no transcendence. Then they once again obey unconditionally, but without the Biblical faith; to us Westerners such a life is completely meaningless.

However, we must keep in mind that the unification of philosophy and theology does not necessarily involve religion. Even if theologians and philosophers were in agreement as to the method of clarifying the Encompassing, there would be no uniformity in religious practice. And it is in the realm of practical religion, in the performance of the rites, in preaching, in interpreting the mythical language, that the minister puts his calling to the test.

IV. BULTMANN'S SPIRITUAL PERSONALITY

Anyone, whether theologian or philosopher, who makes claims which in effect go beyond science, even if they falsely assume a scientific form, must put up with being scrutinized personally. For here issues and personalities are inseparable, casting light on each other.

The discussion about demythologization was touched off by Bultmann, perhaps to his own surprise. His original paper on the subject, "New Testament and Mythology," is the second essay in the book *Revelation and Redemptive History*, published in 1941. It is by no means presented there as being of special importance. Possibly something had been smoldering in the world of theology, and Bultmann's essay merely fanned the flames. Nevertheless the ensuing debate has been stamped by Bultmann's personality to such an extent that we cannot help becoming interested in him.

Bultmann is a historian whose investigations provide us with uncommonly reliable information. He has the rare honesty of acknowledging uncomfortable or awkward facts, as when he wrote this sentence: "Jesus was mistaken." I confess that as a layman I have learned more from him and from Dibelius than from any other contemporary theologian. Bultmann presents his historical studies in a wonderfully clear style, and he holds his reader's interest.

But when Bultmann passes to "existentialist interpretation," as he repeatedly does, he becomes boring as a historian, there is no more to learn from him. At the same time he seems to fail in his objective, or he achieves it only rudimentarily. I don't know whether his views can stir a pastor. At all events they do not stir a man who does not share them out of his own faith. In his existentialist interpretation Bultmann remains learned and argumentative in a scientific fashion. He shrouds the splendors of the Bible with an enveloping layer of dry, objective language. His style is neither ponderous nor light, but conveys an atmosphere of sullen rigidity.

But to note a certain discrepancy between the historian and the theologian is not to play one against the other. Because he is a great scholar we must not expect him to be a good theologian. If—perhaps—he is a bad theologian, one who makes promises that he does not keep, this does not put in question his scientific historical work.

Yet, I suspect that if Bultmann were praised for his honesty, he would take such praise for granted as a natural tribute; he would not be taken aback, he would not reply, for instance: "No man can really succeed in being honest. Though honesty is a human requirement, it is a tremendous one; I am afraid I do not come up to it." Now, there is no doubt that Bultmann is always guided by his honesty when he works scientifically, but it seems to me that his honesty, without his realizing it, is severely strained when he speaks of religion not as a historian but as a theologian. Yet who can be sure in such a matter! Here everyone confronts the mystery of the other, whom he never sees wholly. One can only voice the aspect that was disclosed to one, and not in judgment, but only as a question.

What does Bultmann represent? He is not a liberal and not an orthodox authoritarian. It is quite possible that a naïve piety rooted in childhood memories would not be shaken by his views, for all that they are disintegrating—in my opinion, they are a betrayal of both theology and philosophy. He is influenced by a modern, supposedly enlightened world-view; he speaks as though he could have scientific knowledge of the matters he discusses, so that we are not aware of an appeal to faith and commitment. If this jumble of science and theology represents anything, it is, in the last analysis, orthodoxy. It seems to me a most peculiar mixture of false enlightenment and high-handed orthodoxy.

Combined with his self-assurance regarding scientific method, this no doubt accounts for his unshakable dignity. This would also account for the ease with which he broke off communication with an orthodox adversary, whose views he did not care to discuss at length: "I think that I can settle my dispute with him peacefully, provided each of us makes one concession to the other: I will concede that I do not understand a thing about *Realtheologie*, and he, that he does not understand a thing about demythologization." It is doubtless physically impossible to answer everyone who expresses himself privately or publicly in such a large debate. It is also a fact that dialogue often seems pointless. But the will to communicate, which has its roots in

Biblical thinking, must not break down so readily. Granted, this will must keep silent all too often; but when such silence is combined with a coldness that denounces a radical inability to comprehend in a tone of biting irony, it seems to me indicative of a shut-in obstinacy. We often hear remarks, uttered in the most casual tone, like: "I cannot understand this," or "We shall never understand each other." This casualness is also Bultmann's. To me it seems the hallmark of every orthodoxy, and not only the Christian one.

It would seem that in venturing afield, the great scholar has disappointed both the philosopher whom he leaves without a philosophy, and the minister to whom he actually shows no path at all. For the views Bultmann advances can scarcely be comprehensible to the pastor and his flock. Do they help those who candidly seek self-clarification in a spiritual experience capable of bearing the whole burden of life?

2

THE CASE FOR

DEMYTHOLOGIZATION

A Reply by Rudolf Bultmann

I was at first pleased, indeed, I felt honored when Karl Jaspers expressed himself on the issue of demythologization. But after reading and re-reading his remarks,[1] I found it difficult to reply to them. I feel ever more strongly that they have little in common with the spirit of genuine communication. Their style is not that of a Socratic-Platonic dialogue, but rather of an *ex cathedra* pronouncement.

Jaspers has made it impossible for me to make any answer to a number of things. For were I to defend myself against the criticisms that I am "untouched by the least breath of Kantian or Platonic thinking," that my conception of philosophy is "that of nineteenth-century academicians or Hellenistic doxographers," or that I confuse "genuine enlightenment" with "sham enlightenment," I should seem a ridiculous figure. Nor can I reply to his doubts about how useful my theological work may be to the pastor. As for his characterization of my personality, no one can expect me to comment on that. You don't argue about your obituary.

I shall, moreover, refrain from dealing with Jaspers' criticism of my "assumptions," on which, he says, my theses rest "as upon two pillars." It may become clear indirectly, on the basis of what follows, that I neither hold that modern science provides us with

[1] First published in *Schweizerische Theologische Rundschau,* 1953, No. 3–4, pp. 74–106, and later in *Merkur.*

a "world-view" in Jaspers' meaning of this term, nor do I base my thinking on a philosophical doctrine. Regarding the latter question, I may gratefully refer to the analysis by Kurt Reidemeister,[1] who has shown that demythologization involves a hermeneutic problem arising from a concrete situation, and that in this situation, which is not defined by any special method of philosophizing, the distinction between "existential" and "existentialist" is unavoidable. Further, I can refer to Friedrich Gogarten's work *Entmythologisierung und Kirche* (Demythologization and the Church),[2] which makes it clear that we do not necessarily subscribe to Heidegger's philosophical theories when we learn something from his existentialist analysis. The fact is that Heidegger attacks a problem with which theologians have grappled since Ernst Troeltsch, namely, the problem of history, which has become more acute for theology with every advance in historical understanding of the Bible. Trying to clarify the dependence of human existence on history, and by the same token, on historical comprehension, and going beyond the traditional "subject-object schema," theology is willing to learn from Heidegger. "Needless to say, we may learn from others besides Heidegger. If we can learn those things better elsewhere, it is all to the good. But they have to be learned." And it is true, more generally, that "he who reflects critically on the concepts he uses, whether theological or physical, by the same token comes close to philosophy and utilizes its conclusions" [Gogarten]. Whether theology is advanced or not by its recourse to modern philosophy depends not on arbitrary choice or individual preference, but on the historical situation: for both theology and philosophy have begun to realize how questionable is the thinking that has prevailed in science down to the present time.

Would not a genuine discussion of demythologization have

[1] Published in *Sammlung*, VIII, 1953, pp. 528–534.
[2] Vorwerk-Verlag, Stuttgart, 1953.

to begin by clearly formulating the problem involved? Does Jaspers see this problem? He takes it for granted that I want to salvage faith in so far as it can be salvaged in the face of scientific insights that cannot be ignored; that I want to give the unbeliever "a means to persevere in his faith with a good conscience." Now, this is most certainly not my intention. The purpose of demythologization is not to make religion more acceptable to modern man by trimming the traditional Biblical texts, but to make clearer to modern man what the Christian faith is. He must be confronted with the issue of decision, be provoked to decision by the fact that the stumbling block to faith, the *skándalon*, is peculiarly disturbing to man in general, not only to modern man (modern man being only one species of man). Therefore my attempt to demythologize begins, true enough, by clearing away the false stumbling blocks created for modern man by the fact that his world view is determined by science.

Such an attempt does not aim at reassuring modern man by saying to him: "You no longer have to believe this and that." To be sure, it says this among other things, and may thereby relieve his pangs of conscience; but if it does so, it does so not by showing him that the number of things to be believed is smaller than he had thought, but because it shows him that to believe at all is qualitatively different from accepting a certain number of propositions. It is by striving to clarify the meaning of faith that demythologization leads man to the issue of decision, not by "an intellectual assimilation of existential propositions in the Bible by means of existentialist exegesis," nor by "a new method for the true acquisition of faith" through existentialist interpretation.

It is this—to disclose what the Christian faith is, to disclose the issue of decision—that seems to me the only, the crucial thing that the theologian must accomplish in the face of "the real dangers that threaten us today . . . the deceptive hopes and expectations derived from fear and conceived in helplessness and confusion . . . the facile expedients resorted to by medicine, politics, theology, with uniformly ruinous effects." He must clarify the question that God poses to man, such a stumbling block for the "natural" man, because it entails the sacrifice of all security attainable by his own unaided efforts.

That Jaspers has no clear conception of this stumbling block is shown, on the one hand, by his obvious belief that it consists in Christian revelation's claim to absoluteness (to which we shall return later), and, on the other hand, by his reduction of Biblical faith to trivial "consciousness of the God-created nobility of man" —he even equates this consciousness of the God-given *nobilitas ingenita* with the Biblical (incidentally, Paulinian) "Christ in me"—by his failure to understand the Paulinian doctrine of justification by faith alone without the works of law, and by his opinion that the Gospel according to St. John "mythically justifies the earliest Christian anti-Semitism."

The real problem, in other words, is the hermeneutic one, i.e., the problem of interpreting the Bible and the teachings of the Church in such a way that they may become understandable as a summons to man. But Jaspers, it seems to me, despite his lengthy disquisition on comprehension, has not really grasped the hermeneutic problem. Of course, we cannot reproach him for not having personally experienced the responsibility involved in interpreting a Biblical text. But had we not the right to expect that he would make an attempt to understand this task and the responsibility it involves?

He is as convinced as I am that a corpse cannot come back to life or rise from the grave, that there are no demons and no magic causality. But how am I, in my capacity as pastor, to explain, in my sermons and classes, texts dealing with the Resurrection of Jesus in the flesh, with demons, or with magic causality? And how am I, in my capacity as theological scholar, to guide the pastor in his task by my interpretations? How would Jaspers interpret, say, Rom. 5: 12–21 or 6: 1–11, if he had to? When he says that the redemptive history, which actually is related in the New Testament in the form of a myth (for instance, Phil. 2: 6–11), must "be tested existentially and judged on the basis of the strength that emanates from its language, and the truth that arises from it in the reality of life," I can only reply to such a vague statement by the question, "Well, how is this done?"

The magic word with which he dismisses the hermeneutic problem is "the cipher" (occasionally also "symbol"). The mythological statements in the texts, according to him, are "ciphers," and the mythological language is "a cipher language." What is in cipher? Is it "transcendence," is it the transcendent God? "Myth is the language of reality that is not empirical, but existential." [1]

To define the myth as a cipher of transcendence merely describes the problem of interpretation; it scarcely solves it. All mythologies have this in common (if we set aside the purely etiological myths), that they refer to a reality situated beyond empirical reality, independent of man. But is that reality—and hence human existence—understood in the same way by all

---

[1] Disregarding the question of whether this reality can be expressed only in mythological language, as Jaspers maintains, I should like to ask whether his conception of the myth, in so far as he defines it as a statement in cipher, is so different from my own. When I say that the myth expresses man's knowledge of the ground and limits of his being, is this so different from what Jaspers implies? At all events, I agree with him that the myth is misunderstood when the reality it denotes is conceived of as empirical, and its language as that of "a guaranteed and guaranteeing physical presence." In my opinion such misunderstanding is not accidental; rather it is a characteristic of original myth that in it empirical reality and existential reality are not distinguished. Mythical thinking is just as objectifying as scientific thinking, for instance, when the former represents the transcendence of God in terms of remoteness in space, or when it personifies the power of evil as Satan. This is precisely what makes demythologization necessary.

mythologies? In Indian, in Greek, and in Biblical mythology? Naturally, Jaspers cannot ignore the richness and diversity of the "ciphers." But is this diversity a matter of indifference, in as much as all myths are merely ciphers of transcendence? When Jaspers says that the revelation of truth is "a series of sudden illuminations in the history of the mind," he seems to look upon the diversity of myths as a purely accidental fact, determined by historical concretion.

Or do I misunderstand him? After all, he also says that myths are opposed to myths, and that it is possible to struggle for what we believe to be the true faith within the terms of mythical thinking. Since Jaspers gives no examples, confining himself to the general remark that for us the Bible is the favorite arena for such spiritual struggle, and that another arena is provided by the Greek epic poems and tragedies, and still another by the sacred books of Asia, I cannot imagine how, in his opinion, this spiritual struggle should be fought. Must we not interpret the various myths with regard to the existential understanding expressed in them? Is it only in philosophy that there are existential differences, between Jaspers and Heidegger, for instance, not in mythology, too?

In short, Jaspers does not seem to have grasped the hermeneutic problem or to have taken it seriously. His assertion that assimilation of the mythical language of faith must be effected by transforming the content of the myth itself, by giving it meanings cogent in our own time, tell us nothing at all about what such a transformation may actually be, or what is transformed by it; nor does he tell us what is the element of truth that persists throughout the transformations of the myth.

Jaspers also eludes the hermeneutic problem by denying that the task of interpreting the Bible objectively is the scholar's: he assigns it to the minister who "boldly sets out to understand the language of transcendence (which he conceives of as the language of God) and to speak it himself in his community." Must not the minister, in order to understand the language of the Bible as the language of transcendence and thereby as the language of God, also understand the Hebrew and Greek languages? And if he does not know these languages, must he not rely on scholars who do know them? Does translation into contemporary German amount to no more than transposing foreign words into German ones? Does not the minister need for this purpose a deeper understanding of the language, of its conceptual pattern, of the thinking that guides it? In other words, is not translation always interpretation as well?

Furthermore, must not scholarly translation be "correct" (in so far as this is attainable)? Can the exegete, who strives to comprehend that which was "primarily comprehended" (to use Jaspers' term) understand the primarily comprehended with its "valuations" of good and evil, true and false, beautiful and ugly before he has correctly understood the text? "Biblical faith is not acquired by study," says Jaspers. It certainly is not—but when have I maintained that it was? Comprehension of religion (surely this must mean believing comprehension), Jaspers also says, has nothing to do with scientific method. It certainly has not—yet religious-comprehending appropriation of the Biblical word is possible only when the Biblical texts are translated into a language understandable today. Is such a translation possible without methodical study?

Now, it is true that such methodical study (aiming at "secondary comprehension") is impossible unless a potentiality for primary comprehension is present in the student, i.e., unless he has a primarily comprehending, existential rapport with the subject treated in the text he is to interpret.[1] Therefore, when he wants to show what the text regards as good or evil, true or

[1] Cf. my paper "Concerning the Hermeneutic Problem," in *Glauben und Verstehen,* II, 1953, pp. 211–235.

false, etc., he can do this only if he himself experiences good or evil, true or false, as existential possibilities. This does not prevent him from suspending, i.e., from keeping under question, his own "valuations." Objective interpretation of what is "correct" leads the hearer or reader *indirectly* into the situation of decision. But interpretation itself can only discover and strive to show what is "correct." In so far as it discloses possibilities of existential understanding through indirect appeal to the hearer or reader, it does not deprive him of decision. Naturally it cannot prevent the hearer or reader from misunderstanding what has been said, when he has failed to perceive the appeal.

What is true of every interpretation applies also to interpretation of the Bible. Here, too, what is "correct" can only be discovered and demonstrated when the interpreter stands in definite relation to the matter in question. But this does not imply the impossible requirement that the interpreter should assume that he has faith; what it does imply is that he must be vitally concerned with the existential question, to which faith is a possible answer, though not an answer that can be demonstrated by the interpretation.

Jaspers' failure to understand the predicament of the interpreter seems to me linked with his denial of the possibility of existentialist analysis. Why the latter should be impossible, I cannot see. Certainly, what Jaspers calls "existential clarification" differs from Heidegger's phenomenological analysis of empirical existence in this, that existential clarification is effected only in the act of existing, and is inseparable from "existential communication." But Jaspers cannot help explaining what he calls "existential clarification" in such a way that it becomes universally understandable, i.e., he is obliged to objectify it as a doctrine. And if Jaspers were to claim that the objectification is transcended in genuine (existential) comprehension, much the same could be said of Heidegger's analysis. Heidegger's phenomenological

analysis of empirical existence as self-contained and self-resolved
in Being toward death does not debar anyone, not even those
who are convinced by this analysis as a doctrine, from the existential venture. Rather, it shows that the existential venture is
always personal, and it clearly emphasizes the appeal, which
Jaspers regards as basic, "to selfhood, to authenticity, to actual
being, to a sinking into the original, historical facticity (*Sosein*),
in order to be appropriated—the appeal to earnest questioning
in a hopeless situation."

Whether such propositions of Jaspers as this one: "Everything
is comprehended. . . . Comprehension is the mode of presence
of the Being that we are" are or are not to be termed "existentialist analysis," seems to be a purely verbal question. The same goes
for his statement about "the responsibility of man thrown back
upon himself. It is only through freedom that he experiences
how he is given to himself by transcendence—in freedom not by
freedom." Or his remark that "every man in his freedom has the
possibility of experiencing himself as being given and guided by
transcendence." Were a reader to accept such sentences as a
clarification of his Being, would he be accepting a scientific
philosophy of the kind evolved by "nineteenth-century academicians"? Jaspers, too, it would seem, can be misinterpreted. But
to misunderstand or abuse existentialist analysis is surely not to
demonstrate its impossibility.

In my opinion, Jaspers comes closest to the hermeneutic problem when he reflects on the relation between subject and object.
But if he were interested in a genuine dialogue, i.e., in a joint
search for the truth by means of reciprocal critical questioning,
he could not fail to see that the problem of the relation between
subject and object also motivates my hermeneutic efforts: for my
purpose is to arrive at a genuine comprehension of past existential
insights, a comprehension that would go beyond the horizons
of objectified thinking. I feel that Jaspers misses the point when

he suggests that I am not subjectively committed to my objective conclusions, that in my case "the objectivity of what is said and the subjectivity of the speaker" do not coincide.

For my part, however, I would not agree with Jaspers' view that such a coincidence, when it does take place, is attributable to "the Encompassing"; rather, it occurs when the subject perceives the object as a summons to him in the genuine encounter. To account for it by "the Encompassing" is, in my opinion, not only to engage in superfluous speculation, but also to miss the earnestness of the summons, of the encounter. In Jaspers' thinking the Encounter and the Summon play no part whatever; and as I see it, this means that he has failed to grasp the full importance of the historicity of human existence. In so far as I can judge from his analyses, he understands by historicity merely the fact that man is always situated at a certain point in time, that he lives under accidental historical conditions and is influenced by historical traditions.

For the same reason Jaspers' concept of transcendence seems to me questionable. Transcendence obviously has at first for him the negative sense of the nonobjective; then, the insight that *Existenz* does not belong to the world of objects leads him to hypostatize the nonobjective as the All-Encompassing, indeed, as God. This enables him to speak in the language of myth, which, according to him, is indispensable. Thus he says that man has the possibility of experiencing himself as given to himself and guided by transcendence, and that the liberal faith does not regard it impossible for God, conceived of as absolute transcendence, to effect anything. This All-Encompassing reminds us of the "universum" of Schleiermacher, to whom Jaspers occasionally refers rather maliciously. Other statements remind us of Kant. According to Jaspers, direct relation with the godhead is possible for every man in his own responsible freedom of reason. "In the direct relation of his own freedom to God," man knows that he is determined by God. In the last analysis, what is this transcendence but that which was formerly called "the spirit"?—the spirit which, to be sure, is transcendent in relation to "physical presence," but is immanent in human reason! Is such transcendence the transcendence of God? And since, according to Jaspers, "the mystery of the revelation of the truth" is disclosed in sudden illuminations within the history of the spirit, his transcendence seems also to be immanent in history.

Jaspers' concept of transcendence now leads him to his interpretation of the revealed faith. He says that the belief that "God manifests himself at a given place and time, that he has revealed himself at one place and time and only there and then, makes God appear as a fixed thing, an object in the world." Very true! It is also true that the Christian churches often interpreted and still interpret the revealed faith in that way. But does not Jaspers see that such a conception of the revealed faith has been fought against repeatedly? Does he not know that what I am fighting against is just this fixation of God as an objective entity, against misconceiving the revelation as an act accomplished once and for all? Does he not grasp that the purpose of my demythologization is to interpret the mythological eschatology of the New Testament in such a way that the process of revelation is given its genuine meaning of an "eschatological" process? He may regard my conception as false, but can a genuine dialogue take place if one of its participants ignores the intention of the other?

Now, I have the impression that Jaspers thinks it impossible to have a genuine dialogue with me, on account of what he calls my orthodoxy, or because as a Christian theologian I assert the absoluteness of the Christian revelation. Does Jaspers realize that wherever a revealed faith speaks, it asserts, and must assert, the absoluteness of its revelation, because it regards itself as the true fulfillment of the commandment: "I am the Lord thy God. . . . Thou shalt have no other gods before me." Everyone is free to regard such a revealed faith as absurd. But a man who does, should not talk about revelation. At all events, it is absurd to look for various instances of revelation in the history of religion or the spirit. As a historian I can only discover various instances of faith in revelation, never of the revelation itself. For the revelation is revelation only *in actu* and only *pro me;* it is understood and recognized as such only in personal decision.

It follows that it is also absurd to ask: "How do we recognize revelation? What criterion of truth is given for the direct revelation of God?"—for such questions presuppose that we can ascertain the truth of the revelation before recognizing it as revelation. When we speak of revelation in the true sense of the word, such questions cannot arise, and the impossibility of applying criteria is part of the stumbling block inherent in the revelation. As though God had to justify himself to man! As though every demand for justification (including the one concealed in the demand for criteria) did not have to be dropped as soon as the face of God appears! As though man's justification were not a gift to the man who has fallen to his knees before God! After all, that is the meaning of the doctrine (which Jaspers regards as mythological) of justification by grace alone without the works of law. For "the works" denote here the actions of a man who strives to justify himself before God by his own strength, who boasts and asserts his claims before God.

If this doctrine of justification by faith alone without the works of law is the content of the revelation, then it is true that the Christian faith must assert a revelation "frozen in its definitiveness." Otherwise it could not speak seriously of revelation. It is, however, clear—and I think that Jaspers should have seen this—that this content of the revelation can never be accepted as a doctrine in the sense of an orthodoxy, without at once losing its truth. If this were to come to pass, Jaspers' liberal faith would be perfectly right in refusing "to arrest its movement in time by a revelation frozen in its definitiveness." But after all, revelation is truth only in the event.

Does Jaspers imagine that I fail to realize that "whatever is said and done in the name of revelation" is "said and done in worldly form, in worldly language, in human acts and human perceptions"? After all, the Christian doctrine of incarnation explicitly says this very thing (in mythological language!). What matters is that the incarnation should not be conceived of as a miracle that happened about 1950 years ago, but as an eschatological happening, which, beginning with Jesus, is always present in the words of men proclaiming it to be a human experience.

If the redemptive history were an objective event in a remote past, if it were "an objective redemptive history" in *that* sense, liberal faith would be perfectly right in repudiating it, "as an absolute event and as a prerequisite of salvation for all men." But in the Christian conception, faith is not "weakened" by the denial that historical objectification is absolutely and universally valid, i.e., by the denial that "faith can find objective guarantees in the world." On the contrary, it is only when there is no such objective guarantee that faith acquires meaning and strength, for only then is it authentic decision.

When the revelation is truly understood as God's revelation, it is no longer a communication of teachings, nor of ethical or historical and philosophical truths, but God speaking directly to me, assigning me each time to the place that is allotted me before God, i.e., summoning me in my humanity, which is null without God, and which is open to God only in the recognition of its nullity. Hence there can be only one "criterion" for the truth of revelation, namely, this, that the word which claims to be the revelation must place each man before a decision—the decision as to how he wants to understand himself: as one who wins his life and authenticity by his own resources, reason, and actions, or by the grace of God. The faith that recognizes the claim of the revelation is not a blind faith, accepting something incomprehensible on the authority of something external. For man can understand what the world of the revelation says, since it offers him the two possibilities of his self-understanding.

But we must also say that faith accepts the incredible on authority! For the possibility of living by the grace of God can, by its very nature, be given only to me; it is not a possibility open to all for the taking. If it were, the very meaning of the revelation—the grace given to man who is nothing before God—would be lost. Man does not live by the *idea* of God's grace, but by the grace *actually granted him*.

Thus the revelation has to be an event, which occurs whenever and wherever the word of grace is spoken to a man. The "demythologized" sense of the Christian doctrine of incarnation, of the word that "was made flesh" is precisely this, that God manifests himself not merely as the idea of God—however true this idea may be—but as "my" God, who speaks to me here and now, through a human mouth. And the Christian message is bound to a historical tradition and looks back to a historical figure and its history only to the extent that it regards this figure and its history as evidence of the word of God. The "demythologized" sense of the assertion that Jesus Christ is the eschatological phenomenon that brings the world to its end is precisely this, that Christ is not merely a past phenomenon, but the ever-present word of God, expressing not a general truth, but a concrete message, that word that destroys and in destruction gives life. The paradox of the Christian faith is precisely this, that the eschatological process which sets an end to the world became an event in the history of the world, and becomes an event in every true sermon, and in every Christian utterance. And the paradox of theology is precisely this, that it must speak of faith in objective terms, like any science, while fully realizing that its speaking becomes meaningful only if it goes beyond the "objective" formulation.

For Jaspers, the Christian faith's stumbling block is its claim to absoluteness. Perhaps I should be quite satisfied with the effect my attempt at demythologization has had on him. After all, the purpose of demythologization is to make the stumbling block real. However, I doubt whether I have been successful in this with Jaspers; for I doubt that he has correctly understood the stumbling block. Viewed as an assertion of the absoluteness of the Christian *religion*, it is not correctly understood. As such, it would be meaningless. The Christian religion is a historical phenomenon, as other religions, and like the latter it can be considered with regard to its spiritual content and its existential understanding of man. Certainly, the religions of this earth can be classified from the point of view of their spiritual content and the depth of their existential insight. But even if, in attempting such a classification, we were to give the Christian religion the highest rank, if, for instance, we were to assert its irreplaceable value for human culture, this would mean something fundamentally different from the claim of the Christian faith to absoluteness. This claim can—but also must—be raised by the believer only, not on the basis of a comparison with other modes of faith, but solely as answer to the word that is concretely addressed to me. And this answer is: "Lord to whom shall we go? thou hast the words of eternal life" (John 6: 68).

3

THE ISSUES CLARIFIED

By Karl Jaspers

Your reply contains questions which I am bound to answer; and I wish to comment on your criticisms. The essential ideas of my lecture may be summed up as follows: I regard your demythologization as true to the extent that you deny material reality to the ciphers of religion. But it seems to me that you do not go far enough. For even the word of God can be a mere myth if it is given material reality (incarnated) by being localized at a given place and time in the world, i.e., if it is conceived of as the one truth crucial for man, as God's own action. I went on to attack your concept of demythologization as a whole, in so far as it tends to restrict or even to abolish the field of our mythical thinking as obsolete (modern man's thinking being supposedly determined by modern science). For in my opinion the language of myth is an indispensable cipher of supernatural reality, and to do away with such a language would be disastrous. Finally I assay the differences between us in terms of the opposition between liberalism and orthodoxy, and I conclude that your position can be defined as orthodox. The actual meaning of my lecture, however, was to assert the rights of philosophy.

With your permission, I shall confine myself to those parts of your reply which bear on these basic differences. I should like to elucidate them—possibly they are greater than, possibly not as great as, we think.

1. *The Stumbling Block*

The purpose of demythologization, you claim, is to eliminate the false stumbling blocks that the Biblical ideas constitute to a so-called modern world-view, and to assert the genuine stumbling block of the Christian faith. But you doubt whether I have correctly understood the latter.

Wherein do you see the stumbling block? In the issue of decision. The decision, you say, requires "the sacrifice of all self-sought security." It requires the giving up of "works" conceived of as "the actions of a man who strives to justify himself before God by his own strength, who boasts and asserts his claims before God." According to you, man must decide whether he wants to understand himself, and gain his life and authenticity by his own strength, reason, and action, or "by the grace of God."

If anything like a decision is involved here, it would seem that I am in agreement with you in deciding against exuberant boasting, which is a temptation to all who are successful in life. Further, I confess that it was only thanks to Paul and Augustine that I clearly understoood what had for me been a purely philosophical impulse—the experience of helplessness in freedom. You quote my statements about being given to oneself and losing oneself. This decision is indeed a crucial one for man. But it is reached independently of Christ, independently of a redemptive history I know nothing about, independently of a divine proclamation. The Greek ideas of measure and hybris do not seem to have plumbed this question to its depths. It is idle to ask whether it would have emerged without Paul. It has become separated from Paul, and is now an insight which I regard as philosophically convincing, though not as scientifically cogent. This insight is true, but not because Paul expresses it in a Christian myth.

You say that the purpose of demythologization is to make it clear to modern man what the Christian faith is, and thus to confront him with the question of decision. I have just explained what you mean by this decision. Seemingly or actually I am in agreement with you: only when we are free, and at the same time know that our freedom depends on transcendence—and this dependence is clearly realized only at the peak of freedom—does transcendence speak to us directly, in a way which makes all other speech superficial and indirect. Only this knowledge of our being grounded in transcendence can make us free in the world.

However, the difference between us remains great. First: You say that I reduce the Biblical faith to the trivial idea of man's God-created innate nobility, and that I even equate this nobility with the Biblical "Christ in me." I suppose that in your opinion my triviality is rooted in my conception of evil.

Now, my position is this. To say that man is given to himself, is not to say that he is forgiven sin; what takes place is the awakening of the nobility in man created in God's image and likeness. By being given to himself, man receives unfathomable, unexpected, and incomprehensible help in overcoming evil, which is permanent. To say this is to give mythical expression to a truth which induces man to strive for his self-improvement in repeated and ever-renewed decisions.

I would see triviality only in a conception that tried to talk evil out of existence or that denied its overwhelming power—a power which inwardly we can never rid ourselves of once and for all.

In the idea of grace, I see not only triviality, but a dangerous misconception of God's will (to speak mythically). In the doctrine of justification by faith alone (to the extent that I, as an outsider, understand it at all), the believer is not given to himself in the freedom of his *nobilitas ingenita,* but experiences grace in the forgiveness of sin. On this point I disagree. I persist in believing that through freedom we are able to conquer the strength we need to do good; that in conquering it, we realize that we do not owe our freedom to ourselves, and that we can never entirely and definitively and with certainty free ourselves from error and evil. But such experiences can never be adequately expressed in legal or moral categories of guilt, merit, punishment, grace. The belief that they can be expressed in such categories runs through the Old Testament, and continues in the Christian idea of grace. What formerly had the character of rational calculation, becomes in Christianity an irrational total redemption. The mythical description of God as a judge who condemns and forgives, like all myths, occasionally has meaning and truth. Such mythical ideas can be opposed by other mythical ideas. Thus the doctrine of justification by faith and the idea of grace were opposed by a conception of a transcendent being in which contradictions are brought together, in a God who besides infinite wisdom also contains evil; later Origen denied the reality of the eternal punishments of hell, and, attaining a profundity reminiscent of Asia, saw beyond the superficial façade of religion. But at the superficial level, in thinking that is chained to tangible things, the idea of an eternal hell may again have a limited meaning. In the face of all such ideas, I assert that as a man I can actually be forgiven only by someone whom I have wronged; and that I can assume a guilt that is by definition ineradicable only to the extent that I attempt to do good. However, he who experiences supernatural grace in the forgiveness of sin may express a truth in this myth.

The idea of grace would be somewhat more plausible, if the believers in justification by faith could be regarded as obviously superior to others by virtue of their moral reliability, their saintly lives, and their inner radiance. But what we actually see, physiognomically, as it were, may be considered a consequence of a specifically mythical mode of thinking, in this case, the Lutheran version of the Paulinian doctrines. (Instructive material may be found in Janssen's *History of the German Nation,* which, although written from the Catholic point of view, is an example of how one can learn from one's adversary.)

So much for our difference in the matter of man's innate nobility. Another difference concerning the stumbling block involves the questions of objectivity and absoluteness.

2. *Objectivity and Absoluteness*

You conjecture that I have not understood the stumbling block of the Christian faith, which your concept of demythologization is intended to assert. In your writings, the stumbling block (*skándalon*) seems to denote two different things. First, it means that man takes offense at the idea that he should comprehend his nullity, or that he can be himself only if he is given to himself (we have just discussed this). Second, it seems to mean that we object to the idea that God addressed man only at a given place, in Palestine, nearly two thousand years ago, and that his revelation has an absolute character. While you grant that the revelation is real only as an event in the believer, you maintain that it is objective as divine proclamation.

You say that I fail to understand the purpose of demythologization which is to eliminate objective fixation. You think that I would agree with you if I understood this. But I must ask how you effect this elimination of objectivity.

You fight against the conception of revelation as something that has become public knowledge, against fixation of the content of the revelation in dogma, and you are in favor of the conception of revelation as event. This event, you say, is present in the Word that proclaims it; it is an eschatological event, which, beginning with the historical person of Jesus, has continued to this day. It must not be conceived of as "a miracle that took place about 1950 years ago."

I confess that I still cannot understand such propositions. First, by far the greater part of Christian dogmatics does not agree with you (this would be only a historical, not a material objection). But above all, it seems to me that by asserting that God's summons to decision, or the encounter, still takes place by way of that miracle of about 1950 years ago, you retain the objectivity of the revelation. You say that it is only an event, the word of God conceived of "as my God, who here and now speaks to me through the mouths of men"; but you also say that this event is bound to a tradition and to "its figure and history," which provide us with "evidence of the word of God." This implies that the word of God is bound to the actual words of the New Testament, that is to say, to a completely frozen objectivity.

Obviously this is entirely different from whatever revelation I can have as a man and philosopher, in my direct, non-mediated relation with the godhead in my own reason and freedom. The revelation, as you see it, must reach me from outside, I must perceive it as God's words through the intervention of a specific objective reality.

So far as I can see, this is in contradiction with your intention to abolish the objective fixation. Moreover, it seems to me that your position is incompatible with the Protestant conception of a universal priesthood, according to which man in his relation to the godhead is bound to no mediator, and hence to no mediator of the divine proclamation.

Only by assuming that you recognize a fixed objectivity can I understand your statement that the revelation demands a decision, in the sense that it implies "the claim of Christian faith to absoluteness." This claim, you say, "can . . . but also must . . . be raised only by the believer . . . as an answer to the word of

God . . . And this answer is: Lord, to whom shall we go? Thou hast the words of eternal life (John 6: 68)."

I must confess that once again I do not understand. I ask: Decision for what? For Christ, for that redemptive history begun 1950 years ago? I see no decision involved here. I realize that I am living in a context of Biblical thinking, that I was born in it and breathe it, like all Western men, Jews, Catholics, or Protestants. I consider myself a Protestant, I am a church member, and as a Protestant I enjoy the freedom to ascertain my faith, the faith on the basis of which I like to think I live, without mediators, in direct relation to transcendence, guided by the Bible and by Kant. But none of this, as I see it, involves decision. Where I do see decision is in vital actions, in resolves unswervingly followed. But I have never decided the nature of that within which I find myself, and out of which I believe. I repudiate all creeds that can be formulated in objective terms. When I re-read your reply, I feel that here we agree, and yet I am still forced to conclude that we differ radically.

What is it, then, this disagreement between us? I shall try to put it differently. It concerns the origin of the basic experience we seemingly share, that of man's insignificance and being-given-to-himself. In your case it does not seem to spring from the source that is open to me in my freedom, you do not have it in a radically direct relation with the godhead, but through the mediation of a divine proclamation, which is bound historically to a given place and time. You believe that this revelation began at that place and that time, and that it continues down to this day as an eschatological event. According to you, the decision must be taken in relation to that event.

Have you grasped the implications of such a conception? When, for example, you wrote that the idea of God without Christ is madness? The implications of a faith in which the decision is bound to a divine proclamation conceived of as objective and absolute? The implications of the fact that it must be so conceived? For example, the implication that we others are "poor lost heathen"? The words are not yours. I suppose the thought is not either. But is not this the inevitable consequence of your position?

The difference between us may be clarified by a few more distinctions:

"The stumbling block" is an essential element of philosophical communication, too. But the term means radically different things according to whether it denotes stimulus to belief or communication of belief. This distinction was formulated by Kierkegaard: Socrates is such a stimulus or gadfly; one man cannot give another the truth of faith, he can only make him aware of the truth that is hidden in him. But Christ, each time the Word is proclaimed, gives the faith itself along with the truth, that is, he gives the grace enabling us to believe what has been proclaimed.

You seem to mitigate the stumbling block of faith by distinguishing between the absoluteness of the Christian faith and the absoluteness of the Christian religion. I can understand this distinction only as implying that faith nevertheless justifies the practice of religion in history. Perhaps you have in mind the distinction between the inner and the outer. But, while the idea of an invisible church, a pure Biblical religion, or an absolute faith which becomes event only in the individual, is useful as a signpost, it becomes real only in visible churches, in historically determined denominations, in living individuals. That signpost may be the stumbling block, because it reminds us of what is really essential. But this essential must always be translated into reality in order to exist at all. This much, I think, I can understand. But if that signpost is to function as the stumbling block of the Christian faith, it is no longer a Socratic gadfly. And if that is your meaning when you describe your concept of de-

mythologization as "a parallel to the Paulinian doctrine of justification by faith alone without the works of law," I cannot follow
you. However, even though I find such a doctrine incomprehensible, I can recognize it as identical with certain other Christian
doctrines, which appear to me no less incomprehensible and
terrible, for instance, in Luther.

The difference between the stumbling block as you understand
it, and as a possible philosophy might envisage it, is this, if I am
not mistaken: though you repudiate all objective fixations, you
nevertheless depend upon an objective historical fact, present to
us in the Word, with the result that "the claim of Christian faith
to absoluteness" not only can but also must be raised by each
believer, namely as "the answer to the word of God," which is
the word of Christ. Whereas the philosopher, though depending
unconditionally upon being given to himself in freedom through
transcendence, makes no absolute claim with respect of others.
The truth of your faith claims exclusivity on the ground that it
is based upon divine proclamation. The truth of the philosophical
faith is communicated by words and deeds, becoming in communication a stimulus to others to find themselves by following
similar paths in their own historicity.

You believe that God himself, in the words of the New Testament, poses the question to us, that he poses it to us only there,
and that we can hear it only there. When I ask for a criterion of
the truth of this revelation, you say that such a criterion is to be
found only by comparing this revelation with other revelations.
Such a comparison (between religions, that is) you believe to be
absurd when God himself speaks. "The impossibility of applying
criteria is part of the stumbling block inherent in the revelation.
As though God had to justify himself to man." I would say, no.
It is not God who must justify himself, but every manifestation
in the world that pretends to be the word of God, the act of
God, the revelation of God. You yourself say that everything

is done through men. It is not God who has to justify himself, but Paul and all those who followed him down to Luther, and on to the present. I do not understand how you can regard something human as the word of God, in the sense that it is no longer subject to verification. Wherever and whenever a man claims to speak in the name of God: there is the *skándalon*. It is not God who is to be tested, but whether what a man says is true, and who he is. It is not proud wilfulness that demands such verification, but God himself, through the freedom he has given me, a freedom continuously confirmed by the fact that God remains hidden. He proclaims his will (to speak mythically, but it is a truth men live and die by) that we are not to tolerate it that a man should presume to impose on us, as a revelation of God, an unprovable truth, or that he should demand doctrinal obedience forbidding all contradiction. It is only men who do this.

God speaks quite differently when man reaches an unconditional decision in philosophizing. Despite the peace of mind the decision gives him, he remains uncertain as to whether God's will (to speak mythically) has been done. The proposition, "The voice of conscience is the voice of God" is not absolutely valid: for conscience, too, can deceive. Nowhere do we directly perceive the voice of God; whatever I do or know is always ambivalent. Serenity after decision means only that when I act with a pure will and to the best of my ability, without self-deception, God does not condemn me (to speak mythically). Under no circumstances have I the right to act or speak in the name of God, to claim that God wills my action, that God is against my enemy, were he even the devil himself. The idea of God by which I may live, and which you regard as madness, has great power. The idea of God is ever present, though God himself remains hidden. But the very idea seems to arouse extraordinary passion. It moves us to indignation against blasphemy whenever God is invoked as the God of parties, nations, churches, and individual interest, however noble, in the course of worldly struggles. The foolish question may be asked—and it probably proves our guileless lack of comprehension—as to whether a pious Christian really holds Jesus to be God, when his faith is explicitly and clearly confronted with the alternative (despite all the dogmas about his humanity, the Incarnation, and the Trinity) or considers this to be true only in a mythical sense. The philosopher, as opposed to the critical-historical skeptic, regards Jesus as a historical figure, and sees in Jesus' faith the same calm determination which the philosopher seeks, and the same uncertainty with respect to God's will, which the philosopher experiences. To him, Jesus, a man, represents questioning of God, obedience to God, search for God —i.e., to know God's intentions—a search he carries on although he is already secure in God. To him Jesus represents the over-coming of all human rigidities and presumptions, a breakthrough to truthfulness and love that knew no bounds, one of the great men who have been crucial in determining the course of philos-ophy. But nowhere is the direct word of God to be found. This conception of Jesus is that of the synoptics (prior to the later additions); it is not that of the Gospel according to St. John.

To conclude this discussion of the stumbling block, decision, objectivity, and the claim to exclusivity, I should like to state emphatically that my purpose, here and in what follows, is not to intervene in a theological debate, but to open up some philo-sophical vistas. At the same time I wish to state some themes of my philosophizing.

My premise is this: No one possesses the one truth valid for all. No one occupies a vantage point from which he can survey all truths, from outside, as it were, to compare and evaluate them. Rather, each of us is in the thick of it. We are also en-gaged in a continual spiritual struggle; and the enemies con-fronting each other are seemingly irreconcilable. We do not fully understand our opponents, but we form an idea of the issues at stake, in order to define our positions more clearly.

From this premise, there follows, first, condemnation of the claim to exclusivity, and, second, the wish to find an opponent who should disclose the truth by which he lives.

Hence the philosopher does not want all men to follow him in his philosophizing; rather, he welcomes the existence of the revealed faith, as well as the other elements of religious life—worship in common, prayer, myth, rites, and holidays—and he wants them to express themselves as vigorously as possible.

Even the claim to exclusivity he must deny unconditionally only when it results in actual coercion and intolerance. He also takes part in the practical struggle against those who aspire to seize power in order to destroy their enemies. But the claim to exclusivity that does not lead to such results (though if we are to judge by historical experience it scarcely ever fails to lead to them in the long run) is a reality that the philosopher cannot wish away; rather, he questions it, seeking to restore the interrupted communication. For he does not recognize a single absolute truth, he recognizes only the unconditionality of his own resolve, which is expressed in his life. This resolve is clarified and strengthened in the spiritual struggle that is fought among truths whose sources are ineradicably different, but whose common ground is disclosed by the fact that they bear upon and matter to each other. Every individual achieves inner peace in a resolve grounded in his own historicity; but there is no peace at the level of objective knowledge, where opposing views confront each other.

At this point, however, I shall venture a brief comment on the stumbling block of the Christian faith. It may be argued that the stumbling block (*skándalon*) inherent in the doctrine of justification and redemption is of minor importance, as against the scandalous fact that Jesus, God's representative on earth, suffered the most disgraceful and painful death. The historical reality of a man's death (how gruesome in comparison with the death of Socrates!) in combination with the myth of a god sacrificing himself, is monstrous in itself. You seem to attach no importance to this *skándalon*, which I regard as significant, whereas your stumbling block, which you do not regard as mythical, is not even a stumbling block for me. In fact, it leaves me indifferent, a curious, alien element of Paulinian-Lutheran theology. But He who was crucified is both reality and myth. Indeed, Dibelius said "He who was executed" in order to dispel the false splendor with which the Cross was invested in the course of the Christian doctrine's successive transformations. The story of terrible injustice done to an innocent man, who was put to death like a criminal slave, with its emphasis on the reality of boundless suffering, has cast an illuminating light on the inevitability of all human suffering and on the human capacity for suffering, and it can help preserve us from Stoic apathy. It is *this* stumbling block—like the one inherent in the idea that man is given to himself—that, as I see it, can still be genuine today. We resist it and we respect it; and when this myth speaks to us, we see everything in a new light. It seems to me that you proclaim a false stumbling block, and that you overlook a genuine stumbling block.

3. *In Defense of Mythical Thinking*

To my contention that your concept of demythologization aims at preserving a minimum of faith, namely, the doctrine of justification by faith without the works of law, your reply is: What is in question is not the number of things to be believed, but the nature of the Christian faith. And Christian faith, you say, confronts us with the issue of decision.

My opinion was that this is nonetheless a minimum, whether quantitative or qualitative, and that it could not be accepted by a philosophical faith, if it were made to depend on a redemptive history beginning with Christ. But the main reason for my resistance was that in such a demythologization the richness of religious life and the cipher language of myth are lost. I spoke in defense of mythical expression, which conveys a truth more real and more efficacious than any empirical knowledge.

The question may well be asked: What is myth? What is it that we call mythical? These terms denote a language of images, ideas, figures, and events, all of which point to the supernatural. But this supernatural meaning is present only in the images themselves; when they are translated into mere ideas, their actual meanings are lost. Furthermore, only mythical ciphers of existential import are meaningful; in this, myths differ from empirical realities all of which have equal validity from the point of view of abstract consciousness. Finally, we are not primarily concerned with myths as objects of historical study, but as presences, as legitimate modes of existential insight.

While the revelation may be distinguished from myth, in my opinion both belong to the reality of the myth. The revelation, too, speaks in terms of a supersensory reality.

Your proposition that mythical thinking is just as objectivizing as scientific thinking—when, for instance, it conceives of God's transcendence in terms of remoteness in space, and personifies evil as Satan—does not apply to this domain of ever-present and eternally meaningful myths. In your opinion, such objectivizations make the task of demythologization necessary. But mythological objectivity is completely different from scientific objectivity. For the reality of the myth is not empirical, i.e., it cannot be investigated in the world. In myth no conscious difference is originally made between empirical and supernatural reality. Where supernatural reality is regarded as tangible empirical reality and nothing else, we no longer have mythical thinking, but materialism, which assumes various historical forms. However, once we become conscious of the difference, we no longer interpret myth in terms of empirical reality, though the language of mythical reality does not necessarily lose its force thereby. Then, the unclear wavering between reality and meaning ceases, and we become aware of the myth as a cipher, as a legitimate means of insight.

You do not approve of the mythical representation of God's transcendence as remoteness in space, or of the mythical division of the world into an upper and a lower region (heaven and hell). Surely you do not think that the vivid images of an upper and a lower region, of nearness and distance, have become obsolete, that they are completely accounted for by so-called psychology, and that they have lost all meaning? These images by which we live have extraordinary symbolic resonance. Several decades ago I was told a story about a physician who asked his wife (she was about to die) how she envisaged death. She replied: The Assumption of the Virgin. Must we conclude that she supposed that a soul, when it quits the body, flies into the upper air first, then to the orbit of the moon, and finally reaches some place that astronomers will eventually discover? Such a notion would have been regarded as nonsense in any epoch, but it may be truer, because it expresses another kind of truth than empirical knowledge about the solar system and the cosmos.

Since the myth does not concern itself with the objective reality of the empirical world, at a certain point it explicitly eliminates empirical reality. Just as metaphysical visions disclose their truth—and this is the case with all great metaphysicians—only after they have been logically reduced to tautologies, circles, or contradictions in terms, so mythical ideas disclose their truth only after having been divested of their empirical reality. And just as metaphysical constructions enjoy a momentary life when the concepts they use seem to correspond to something objective, so mythical ideas are alive when for a moment their content seems to refer to empirical realities.

You deprecate the term "cipher" as a "magic word," by means of which I am supposed to dismiss the hermeneutic problem. You ask: Ciphers of what? My reply is: In this context, the meaning of the cipher is that through it I actually become aware of something that cannot be expressed in any other language. But here the term "language" itself is only a simile (what I understand by "cipher" is expounded at length in the third volume of my *Philosophie*). According to you, this is a meaningless reply, merely describing the problem of interpretation, not solving it. But there is no problem of interpretation here. We interpret intended meanings, as far as possible. But interpretation has become a vice. Within the world as ciphers, it is necessary to perceive directly, to move about as easily as in the world of fairy tales. Interpretation is ruinous unless it is assimilative comprehension, and unless it results in turn in an authentic speaking in ciphers. To enter the world of ciphers we must first experience them deeply in all freedom; then, at a given moment, a cipher becomes the symbol of a reality that cannot be expressed in any other way.

I wrote that in the world of ciphers, i.e., in the world of myths, a constant struggle is taking place. You deplore the absence of examples in my lecture. In this struggle, I said, the existential meaning and the truth of the myth are tested. To such "vague statements" you reply by asking, "How is this done?"

My answer to this question is: You are asking for a recipe. It cannot be done at all. It is as though, being confronted with an elucidation of the loving struggle in communication, or with a hymn to love, you were to ask: How is this done? I am sure your question is not asked maliciously, but it seems to be asked on the pedantic assumption that the issue of demythologization can be discussed in the spirit of a scientific seminar, where everything is reducible to a common-sense methodology.

"How is this done?" The question (which, so formulated, is incidentally blasphemous with regard to the struggle within the domain of myth) might be answered by referring, for instance, to the significant transformations the gods undergo in the *Eumenides* or the *Prometheus* of Aeschylus. Or, by reference to the struggle the Biblical prophets carried on against magic, opposing to it the idea of God. Or, to the changing images of God in the Bible, down to the image of a faintly rustling wind. A struggle within mythical ideas seems to be taking place between you and your opponents on the question of justification by faith alone. As for my own resistance to this myth, I understand it, like so many others, only from afar, but to the degree that I understand it at all, I know that I am repelled by it because it does not clarify anything I hold to be essential, and because when I try to understand its implications, I find myself wandering down paths I do not care to tread. The situation is the same in a quite different field of mythical thinking, namely, in Fichte, when he outlines his myth of the German *Urvolk* in his *Speeches to the German Nation* and draws his conclusions. Any reader, but especially a young one, might be caught up in the ideas and images, and be deeply moved, until it suddenly dawns upon him that he has been led astray by the devil himself. As you can see, it is possible to speak about the struggle within the domain of myth only when a poet-philosopher enlightens us by means of words and brilliant images, or when a thinking philosopher speaks of such phenomena in detail and makes them present to us in specific contexts. It is impossible to speak about these things briefly.

You ask, What is the element that persists through the transformations of the myth. This can be stated only in formal terms: the supernatural in the sensory. What the former is, no representation and no concept can show. But all of us undergo transformations, more or less. It is the external trappings that are transformed, but in such a way that with their transformation the inner meanings are also modified. Occasionally, a core of permanent meaning appears, as in Yahweh's saying, "I am that I am." But the totality of the supernatural contained in mythical thinking will always be beyond our grasp.

What must be kept in mind, however, is that in trying to salvage mythical thinking, we are not motivated by the idea that in the myth we possess the absolute. On the contrary, mythical language always has an uncertain character; all we can say is that the mythical ciphers may in a given situation correspond to existential possibilities. Goethe's saying that as a student of nature he is a pantheist, as a poet a polytheist, and that whenever his moral personality is involved, it too is provided for, expresses most concisely how we can live in a world of possibilities, each of which is actualized at a given moment, thus becoming clear to itself in the language of myth and confirmed in it.

Because of the uncertainty, and hence untruth, which clings to all mythical truth, and which breaks through in every absolutization, it must be said very emphatically in conclusion to these considerations: the whole of mythical, as well as speculative, thinking is transcended in the inexorable commandment: Thou shalt not make unto thee any graven image or any likeness. Since, as finite sensory rational beings we cannot think otherwise than in terms of objects and guided by our senses, the commandment can only mean that we are not to posit as absolute any idea, any mythical figure, any representation of events or entities. It is always the language of transcendence, limitlessly rich, that clarifies meanings at all levels; it is never the transcendence itself. The idea of God, taken seriously, excludes definite determinations, and requires that we go beyond all languages, but only after having passed through them. In the moment that is eternity, we surmount them, having attained the incommunicable imageless. I presume that the minister active in the living faith will not forget any of the levels, will keep them all in a state of proper indeterminateness, and attach them to the single incommunicable point: the infinite.

When I try to read your expositions of justification by faith, especially those in your books, it seems to me that you speak in a foreign language, but that you are going in the same direction as I. It seems to me that you are at home in imagelessness, but that you are asserting it in a way that I cannot understand. However, I shall not be so bold as to say this is the case, because such a statement would seem absurd in view of your actual formulations.

4. Comprehension

A reader of our discussion might say: We are dealing here with things regarding which no decision is possible, indeed, it is not even possible for the opponents to understand each other clearly. Therefore, this question is meaningful: What are we presupposing in our polemic? What is our common ground, without which no dialogue is possible? Your answer to this question is the same as mine: this common ground is comprehension. Even champions of opposing views can adopt a common method of comprehension, and on this point it should be possible to arrive at an agreement sooner than on any other point—an agreement that does not exclude different views.

Now, we do not agree on this point, either. According to you, despite my "long disquisitions on comprehension," I have not grasped the hermeneutic problem, and you ask how I interpret texts and appropriate their meanings.

The problem of the correct comprehension of texts is surely one that can be discussed scientifically. Correctness implies that the one who comprehends discovers the meaning intended by the author of the text. Scientifically, we try to elicit the "facts of the case," i.e., what the author of the text wanted to say. You know the procedure from your studies far better than I do. You say that the correctness striven for should be achieved as far as possible, though the task in question can never be completed. Far-reaching results have been achieved with the help of refined methods of critical interpretation, which were first applied to the Greek and Latin classics and later to the Biblical texts (Spinoza is an early example). I think that up to this point I am in agreement with you.

However, in trying to comprehend meanings we meet with a difficulty that is fundamentally different from any difficulty involved in sensory perception of things. Comprehension can never be completed, not only because its objects are infinite in number, but because of the very nature of its object. For it presupposes in the man who comprehends, qualities which obviously are not possessed by all men, in the way that they all possess faculties of sensory perception or rational understanding. According to whether the meaning to be comprehended is a mathematical insight, an observation of nature, political motives, a mythical vision, or a doctrinal content, different qualities are presupposed in the one who comprehends. Such qualities can be acquired by a rational effort, by mere learning, or are present existentially in a given man; each case implies a radically different mode of comprehension. If the old proposition, "The same is known only by the same," were absolutely valid, the area of comprehension would be confined to the existential area of the comprehender, to that which he himself is. But if there were also a comprehension of that which I am not—the possibility of which is nevertheless inherent in man—i.e., if "I can understand Caesar without being Caesar," then the area of comprehension must be unlimited. Then we could experience possibilities alien to ourselves, without transforming ourselves. Now, there can be no doubt that there have been virtuosi of comprehension, men who seem completely dissimilar from what they have comprehended. Regarding such comprehension, we may mention the unsurpassed (though today largely forgotten) studies by Boöckh, Droysen, Dilthey, Simmel, and, above all, Max Weber, as well as the world of hermeneutics that Joachim Wach treated historically in his work on comprehension.

The term "comprehension," in the sense used by a great scholarly tradition, has today become confused with a new usage which has imperceptibly come to be accepted and even encouraged, as it seems to me, by certain theologians. The term "comprehension" is used in a double sense. In order to make this ambiguity explicit, I distinguished between "primary" and "secondary" comprehension. I do not particularly care for these terms, but I have coined them to avoid the confusion of the present usage.

In primary comprehension, our minds are totally involved; that which was formerly called "comprehension" must now be called "comprehension of the comprehended," or "secondary comprehension." When Caesar crossed the Rubicon, he comprehended the Roman republic, the world situation, and what he had to do about it, all in one act. What he said about it himself, was intended to contribute to the success of his undertaking. But historians have the endless, never-completable task of comprehending what he comprehended. Whereas primary comprehension involves the grasping and the producing of a meaning, the carrying out of an idea, and requires actual contact and identification with that which is comprehended, secondary comprehension involves no such commitment; it operates in the area of the possible, not necessarily involving decision. It serves to achieve the meaningful orientation which is an indispensable condition of freedom, clarity, and knowledge, but which is not real itself.

If our radical distinction between primary and secondary comprehension is valid, the following question acquires a clearer meaning: Where is the boundary of scientifically correct secondary comprehension?

Clearly, it no longer lies in the area of the meaning that was originally intended, if that original meaning is analyzed and developed. For it is possible to draw consequences from a given idea, which were not drawn originally. We may try to determine what Caesar should have comprehended, as distinguished from what he actually comprehended; and we may accept his actual comprehension as true and morally good, or reject it as false and evil, or we may refrain from judging it at all.

Such analysis of the objects of primary comprehension are inherent in our interest in the past. These analyses vary with the character of that interest. But it is clear that our interest in the past always goes beyond the object of primary comprehension, although we ourselves often lag behind the primary comprehension.

However, though the boundary of the historically correct remains undetermined, the methodical goal of our investigations is "historical correctness" in contrast to "factual correctness." And if historically correct results are achieved by this method, it is clear that the historical correctness of the comprehension has no bearing on the truth of that which is comprehended.

Now, such considerations unfortunately oversimplify things. For the objects of secondary comprehension include a wide range of things very different from each other—mathematical insights, observations of nature, philosophical speculations, mythical visions, and so on. The personal qualities required, the methods and arguments used, and the motives of the investigators differ from case to case.

It seems that it is possible to discuss scientifically the correctness of a given instance of secondary comprehension and to arrive at conclusions. Historical science is based on that possibility. But is it also possible to reach agreement concerning the basic forms of primary comprehension?

You quote my statement: "Everything is comprehended. . . . Comprehension is the mode of presence of the being that we are." My formulation followed contemporary usage. Primary comprehension was discussed by Kant in relation to its form and content (designated as faculties of the human reason or the soul), by Hegel (as the manifestations of the spirit), as well as by others. Kant and Hegel, though radically different from each other, seem to me so far unsurpassed in the simplicity of their basic approach and in richness of ideas.

5. *Transcendental and Existential Clarification. The Encompassing. Subject and Object. The Godhead in the Encounter*

Clarification of the forms of primary comprehension is, however, entirely different from clarification of existential possibilities. To elucidate the forms of objectivity, the forms of empirical existence, and the forms of possible *Existenz* (the categories of freedom) is one thing; to speak of man's insignificance, of being given to oneself, of innate nobility, is another. To understand this difference, we must have recourse to that branch of philosophy which has been termed philosophical logic or transcendental philosophy. In my opinion, true philosophy must distinguish between a type of thinking that makes possible a logical community among men, and an existential clarification which is directed at individuals and at the same time separates them at the level of communication. The basic forms of empirical existence—the spirit, possible *Existenz,* abstract consciousness—

are dealt with by a branch of philosophy, in which, unlike matters of faith, rational discussion, and agreement may be possible. But so far such agreement has not actually been achieved; despite the simplicity of the basic ideas, the matter is a complex one. Be that as it may, the issue involved in our discussion concerning matters of faith is something entirely different from what is involved in a discussion on the nature of primary comprehension.

You distinguish between "existential" and "existentialist." You strive to gain insight into the existential by means of existentialist analysis.

Against this I assert: There is a radical difference between a clarification of the fundamental forms of the Being that we are, and a thinking that points to possible *Existenz* by clarifying possibilities. Clarification of the fundamental forms of Being begins with propositions such as, "All our empirical existence is comprehending empirical existence"; "Comprehension is the mode of presence of the Being that we are"; "Everything that happens to us is governed by the conditions of the transcendental faculties of our soul"; "Everything that is, is a manifestation of the spirit in some particular form"; "What is for us, is in consciousness"; "What is, is thinking," and so on. All these formulations deal with one and the same thing, but each of them presupposes a fundamental conception. We do not get out of this circle, we can only try to enlarge it.

Now, the clarification of the fundamental forms also helps us to find our way in an area, in which other philosophical ideas may develop, ideas that by their movement awaken possible *Existenz.*

Unlike the fundamental modes of presence of the Being that we are, what has been called *Existenz* since Kierkegaard cannot become the object of a doctrine. Kierkegaard's theory of "stages," for instance, does not deal with universally valid knowledge, but with decisions of an uncommonly meaningful kind, which open horizons that clarify and confirm these decisions, but do not provide us with a knowledge that every man who understands it must recognize as valid. The unrivaled depth of Kierkegaard's insight consists in this, that into his analyses he builds explosions that undo them, and that by means of indirect communication—in spite of some obvious aberrations, which arise almost inevitably as a result of objective formulation —he was able to say the most illuminating things.

What cannot be obtained by means of existentialist analysis, but only by transcendental clarification, seems to me a great deal. I shall mention only one point, which has a bearing on our discussion:

Without objectivization there is no consciousness. While I am awake, I arrive at clarity only when I have some object before my eyes or before my thought. But each object implies a subject. Although each can, to some extent, be separated from the other, it is always at the cost of truth, whether in favor of a mere objectivity—to which our object then belongs only as a mere point common to all consciousness—or in favor of a mere subjectivity, to which no valid object belongs, and which for that reason withdraws into the darkness of each individual's self, leading to confusion.

Object and subject belong together. This fundamental feature of our empirical existence, of our consciousness, and of our possible *Existenz* I call the Encompassing. Each subject implies the object proper to it, and vice versa. Abstract consciousness, the "I think," implies the valid objectivity of scientific knowledge, in which the common point of consciousness, the "I think" becomes meaningful; empirical existence implies an environment; existential freedom implies transcendence. In each case we must arrive at a subjectivity that is equivalent to its objectivity. Therefore, the propositions "subjectivity is the truth" and "objectivity is the truth" are both valid; neither excludes the other, but requires it as its complement.

Now, you recognize that the objectivity of what is said must be at one with the subjectivity of the speaker, and that we must not isolate one aspect and play it against the other. Whenever we deal with something that has been said, we are entitled to ask: Who is speaking? and, What kind of objectivity is meant? The obvious answers: "Such and such an individual," and "There is only one objectivity" are false. You pass over in silence my classification of both aspects in the modes of the Encompassing— abstract consciousness, empirical existence, the spirit, and *Existenz* —but you condemn my procedure as superfluous speculation. True enough, my lecture could not adequately inform you about my investigations of these things, which I have expounded in my books (particularly in *On Truth* and *Reason and Existenz*).

If you equate my idea of transcendence defined as the All-Encompassing, with Schleiermacher's *universum*, and even with the concept of the spirit (in the sense of the world of culture), it is because you are unacquainted with my writings. I do not think it is possible to assert transcendence more resolutely than I have done in these works. I need not go into this here. My propositions remind you of Kant. There is no tribute I would rather be paid, if it is for the right reasons. I shall not go into this matter, either.

The question of the objectivity of transcendence in relation to possible *Existenz* implies the special question concerning the personality of the godhead. This is not a question of transcendental philosophy but of existential experience, which we can try to grasp by existential clarification, but which cannot be defined in universally valid concepts. You reproach me for ignoring the earnestness of the summons, of the encounter. I will not contradict you on this point, all I can say is: The fact is, I know a Thou, I know a summons and encounter only among men.

From the texts of the past only men speak to me, and these texts tell me something of their state of mind. I cannot deny that transcendence may be experienced as a Thou. For a finite being, which arrives at itself only in a dialogue with a Thou, the fiction of such a Thou as a cipher of transcendence at climactic moments of inward clarity ("and then one became two") is philosophically legitimate. Such an experience is marvelous indeed. But I believe that it also has its dangers. He who has found his God can so easily withdraw from communication in the world. He is not obliged to, but we may observe that such things have happened. If you question my thinking on the ground that I do not realize the seriousness of the encounter with the godhead, I question your thinking on the ground that you do not realize the seriousness of communication among men.

6. *Historicity*

You say: the fact that God speaks to us, that the encounter with the divine Thou plays no part in my thinking, suggests that I do not fully grasp the historicity of man. I reply: the term "historicity" is used in different senses. The diversity of men, nations, and cultures, of myths and religions, of modes of thinking, the life of each individual man from his origin on, in specific situations and with specific opportunities, his dependence on these conditions—all this can be investigated ad infinitum, and remains unsurveyable as a whole. Let us call it "the historical." Now, everyone finds himself in it, but it is not merely by orienting himself in terms of the historical world and of his own origin that he determines exactly where he stands. (Such an orientation would lead to a false anticipation of total knowledge on the basis of a few external indications, and a measure of comprehension.) Rather, individual man finds himself in such a way that he takes himself over as himself in his given reality, makes his decision, and follows it resolutely; and he thereby reduces all external directives for orientation to means, reaching beyond them by his awareness that what is eternal is decided in time. Such a paradoxical expression is unavoidable in this case, if serious commitment is not to lose its character of a manifestation of freedom in time, become a mere object of knowledge, and thus destroy itself. In my *Philosophie* (Vol. II) I called "historicity" not the historically particular, not any given individual or knowable. Rather, I meant by historicity the existential possibility of achieving and experiencing the actual unity of time and eternity in the moment. This possibility is grasped out of existential freedom. Only in this historicity can the merely historical acquire an existential meaning.

But if there is no historicity without the divine Thou, then it is true that I know nothing of historicity.

The historicity of *Existenz* is present in the pious soul without being expressed in concepts. It is the unconditionality of *Existenz* in the historicity of its freedom, which is bestowed on it in the decision by transcendence and fulfilled. But if historicity is clarified historically, two consequences follow for knowledge and by the same token for criticism. First, I realize that the historical contents of religious doctrines and of myths have no universal validity, and I recognize the validity of beliefs that others, in their relation to transcendence, have to regard as true. Second, I see that universally valid knowledge (which achieves its pure form in the sciences) depends on its presuppositions and methods, that each of the possibilities of this knowledge, even the seemingly most universal ones, are particular, and have no bearing on *Existenz*.

From the point of view of philosophical thinking the objectivity of transcendence cannot be conceived as unique, present in the world, subsisting in isolation. Being an individual truth which transforms the man who experiences it, it cannot be truth for all men. What happens to such a man is historical and can awaken us historically, but is not universally valid on the phenomenal level, precisely because it is historical.

Now, it is true that you say: only as an eschatological event, for the believer is the revelation real; it is not real in the sense of a teachable content of revelation. But you also say: God's own words which come to us through the mouths of men are spoken here and nowhere else, and for this reason lay claim to absoluteness, confronting every man who is reached by the divine proclamation with the issue of decision.

Once again I ask, What kind of objectivity is being invoked here? It is supposed to be God Himself. And I ask, For what subject is the divine proclamation valid? For the subject to whom the ability to believe is communicated, thanks to grace, at the same time as the word of God?

But how about those on whom this grace is not bestowed, and who nevertheless perceive the words of the divine proclamation? I can only say this: It is by no means true that such men, who do not feel that they must make a decision, are guilty of defiance, pride, rebellion against God, turning away from God, or whatever other charges may be made against them. Those upon whom that grace of which they hear without understanding is not bestowed, are nevertheless able to perceive the words as ciphers, they may even be stirred by them, and can choose to operate with them in mythical thinking for the purpose of clarifying their experience.

The question of Christian decision in your sense—as I have learned it, not least from you—is, unlike the reality of Jesus' life and message, a theological addition made shortly after Jesus' death. What Jesus places before us is only the question of moral decision in relation to God, a question which bears upon our actual conduct. The philosopher recognizes that Jesus poses this question with extraordinary poignancy, but he recognizes also that the same question is raised by the prophets of the Old Testament and by great philosophers. According to you, the issue of decision is narrowed down to our attitude toward the word of God as it was uttered through the mouths of the primitive Christians. In the eyes of the philosopher, when you make such an assertion, you are confusing a fixation which claims universal validity for an objective historical manifestation, with historicity. Likewise, you confuse the cipher of a supernatural reality, for instance, as it speaks to us uniquely and unforgettably in the descent of the Holy Ghost, with the reality of a historical event. The philosopher must acknowledge his own limitations, as well as the limits of his ability to comprehend. But he knows himself no less determined by God's will (a mythical expression for the ground of his own will and sense of necessity, which cannot be justified rationally) than the theologian. The philosopher, however, unlike the theologian, cannot refer to God or claim to be God's deputy.

7. *The Minister*

In our day the Christian tradition seems to be propagated primarily by three agencies—theology, the church, and the ministry. Now, it seems to me, as a mere observer, that the theologians' work is indispensable for passing on knowledge, but that they cannot tell the ministers "how they should do it," to use your phrase. The church is indispensable organizationally, but is always dangerous, and, most of all, unreliable. It is the ministers who awaken and confirm the actual reality of religious life. Everything depends on them. I permitted myself a few observations on this score, which did not meet with your approval—observations on the need fully to restore the mythical language, on the importance of a historically correct comprehension of the Bible for the actual believer, on the interpretation of Biblical texts by the minister.

What has historically correct comprehension to do with the actual believer? My answer is: almost nothing. Kierkegaard said that study of the New Testament does not further faith in any way, and that all we need is one proposition, namely, that God was made man and was crucified to redeem our sins. If I remember correctly, a theologian, Kähler, expressed a very similar view in a pamphlet I read a long time ago. As a philosophical observer I do not share such radical views, and that is why I said "almost nothing," rather than "nothing." For when you ask whether the minister should know Hebrew and Greek, whether he should read scientific studies of the Bible, my answer will be affirmative, though for reasons different from yours. First, it is desirable that the ministry should be at home in Western culture: it should be acquainted with science, it should help to realize the idea of the university, and its education should be broader than that given in the seminaries. Second, it seems to me that objective historical knowledge of the Holy Scriptures, used as a guide in imparting great truths, enables the minister to express his faith with greater ease. However, he is not bound by the historical knowledge he possesses; it actually frees him to present the objectivized contents of religion in a form that makes them more plausible to his contemporaries, and he thus presents them more effectively. What matters most, is the example of the minister's life and the seriousness of his utterance.

Referring to my observation that myths remain valid even though I do not believe in the resurrection of the body, in demons, or in magical causality, you ask the question, How is this done?—"How would Jaspers interpret, say, Rom. 5: 12–21 or 6: 1–11, if he had to?" Do you mean, How would I speak about these things were I a pastor?, or How would I treat them were

I a theologian and historian of religion? I am neither, but I shall try to put myself in their place. In my capacity as scholar, I would, if I had the skill, try to collect the materials, contemporaneous or earlier texts of related content—as you do in the critical-historical parts of your works—in order to understand, as clearly as possible, the meaning intended by the author. Like you, I would study the use of words. I would not acquire religious insight by this method, but I would at least familiarize myself with a content of faith. I would not attempt an existentialist analysis, i.e.—in so far as I can make out your intention, which seems to me impossible of realization in terms of research—attempt a "translation" into some meaning for which I should expect to find the guiding idea in my philosophical conception of man and the world. In my capacity as pastor, I would go about this quite differently. To be sure, I would read what the scholar has contributed to the "correct" understanding of the intended meaning—the sort of thing I find in your books. But then I would put it all aside, and without being bound by what Paul actually meant, I would proceed on another principle altogether, which I justify approximately as follows: for the last 1,500 years the Western world has regarded the Holy Books as its spiritual guides; and what matters here is not their historically established accuracy, but the spirit of the faith. (You are far better acquainted than I am with the discussions concerning the letter and the spirit, particularly within the domain of Protestantism.) The only essential thing is to speak in such a way that, with the help of a text, a present content of faith should be disclosed, and be shared in communication. For this, the mythical language is as indispensable as is philosophical speculation, depending on the kind of people to whom one speaks. How this is done, is shown, when it is genuine, by the specific actions of a given pastor at a given time and place, in relation to given people. Even today, the Bible is the book most often printed, a book with which nearly a hundred generations of our ancestors lived; even men who do not recognize its sacred character agree that it is a work to be revered. Therefore, this book has the distinction that we need not be concerned with its historical and critical accuracy, any more than former generations were. A philosophical thinker will have the same attitude toward myths (though I should consider this method entirely unjustified with regard to philosophical texts, for such texts command no adherence from a religious community, are not sacred, and when their meanings are appropriated and transformed, they must, by their very nature, make us aware of this transformation). I must forbear, both for lack of space and by reason of my insufficient pneumatic powers, to interpret those Biblical passages for you in such a way as to disclose in them ideas without reference to Paul. Some extraordinary ideas can, I am sure, be developed even on the basis of the Gnostic myths. If I hold myself back, it is not to compromise myself unnecessarily. I may add this much: I would not leave out even resurrection of the dead, demons, or magic, if I could deal with these myths in such a way that it would occur to none of my listeners that they are empirical realities, and if they illumined something that would remain lost without such images.

8. *Science and Philosophy*

In my lecture I formulated theses directed against your theses, which I restate here: There is no such thing as a modern world-view; what you call "the scientific features of the modern world-view" is nothing but what has existed for thousands of years in materialist, sensualist, and realistic thinking; the scientific superstition, which is universal today, has scarcely anything to do with modern science, except for the fact that a small part of that science so impresses by its technological results, that the scientific superstition finds in it the strongest support; finally, by applying technological thinking to actions and modes of conduct that cannot be the object of technological manipulation, the scientific superstition leads to harmful results analogous to the perennial curse of magic. You do not care, you say, to go into these matters. For my part, I would need much more space than I have at my disposal here to document your conception by quotations from your writings, and to make clear what I have said elsewhere about modern science, and on the basis of which your error seems to me demonstrable. That is, I do believe that it is possible to advance cogent scientific arguments in favor of this assertion.

Our debate clearly reveals the difference between rational discussion of a specific subject, i.e., scientific discussion, and an entirely different kind of discussion that is concerned with vital matters. Only in the former case do we have the precision of rational thought, expressed in definitions and in unambiguously formulated questions. In the latter case, we can attempt to clarify ambiguous ideas, but definite formulations are possible only if the opponents have actually been in agreement in advance. Rational discussions aim at conclusions which can be accepted as valid by the abstract understanding; in discussions concerned with matters of faith, it is possible to convey inner dispositions, claims, and decisions, to express one's own views and to reply to questions. In the former, the medium is the definiteness of the universally valid; in the latter, a community of diverse existential possibilities, which cannot be directly ascertained. In the former, thought can be cogent, in the latter, it can only point the way.

If we call science that which is cogently knowable for every understanding, and which for that reason has actually gained universal recognition, then neither philosophy nor theology can be called sciences. But if we call science any thinking that proceeds methodically, seeking to acquire a systematic character, and using (among other means) the rational means of understanding, the situation is different. I regard it as essential, as right and desirable, particularly today, to use the term "science" in the narrow sense, in contrast to the older usage, and not to permit even the beginning of a confusion between the two kinds of knowledge in question. This applies above all to the difference between objective knowledge and religious knowledge.

The fact that you have not been inclined so far to accept, both theoretically and practically, the concept of science in the narrow sense it has acquired only in the modern world (the Greeks arrived at such a concept only on isolated occasions) can be seen from the following instance, among others:

When you say that "theology and philosophy have begun to realize how questionable is the thinking that has prevailed in science down to the present time," you touch upon, I think, a very doubtful subject. Nothing is more certain and more conscious of its methodology than scientific knowledge in its pure form. Its existence is one of the splendors of our age. If many scientists —not science—are dominated by questionable thinking, this is because of their bad philosophy, which falsely refers to science as its foundation. This philosophy has its historical ancestors (among them Descartes) and is rooted objectively in natural misinterpretations of scientific insights. But since you refuse to discuss these things, and since I cannot convince you by brief arguments, I shall confine myself, in order to suggest what I have in mind, to a wish that may seem ridiculous: That your historical works, which even to a layman like myself seem excellent, could be cut in two, as it were. Then we could isolate the parts dealing with matters that can be critically investigated; as for the rest, we could present it in a form different from religious knowledge, the comprehension of faith, existentialist interpretation, or whatever else you may call such appropriating knowledge.

What philosophy is, cannot be determined scientifically. Philosophy is an act of freedom, and determines itself, not by arbitrary caprice, but out of the necessity of a faith that expresses itself in its thinking, out of total vision and will. But the name of philosophy is also borrowed by a so-called "scientific philosophy," which claims to deserve professional status, to achieve progressively increased insight, and to put its results at the disposal of those who need them. I do not deny that there is an immense literature of this type. But I find only a very limited amount of usable material in it, and I note that there is no fundamental or clear agreement as to its boundaries.

I refer to the logical, primarily transcendental-logical analyses (mentioned above), i.e., explorations of the necessary forms of human experience. It is true that such analyses have not so far arrived at universally valid scientific truths. These philosophic insights, too, have a character different from scientific knowledge. But when we move within this area, we nevertheless look for universally valid knowledge, and we believe that here we can operate rationally with ideas accessible to everyone. But a clear boundary between such a knowledge of the universal forms of experience, and, say, the intellectual operations of existential clarification or of metaphysics, has not yet been drawn.

I have ventured to philosophize in a field, where it is easy rationally to destroy all propositions as soon as they are conceived of objectively and if the matters they deal with are conceived of as something that can be scientifically investigated, and eventually known with certainty. In this field I have encountered your concept of demythologization. You operate in this field whenever, in the name of demythologization, you reject ideas that seem to you untenable, whenever you pose the question of decision, whenever you strive to make room for a Christian message in a sense you have made your own.

This discussion must come to an end. True, I believe I have repeatedly recorded our points of contact. But there remains a background regarding which mutual understanding is difficult, though some minor misunderstandings might be clarified and removed without further ado.

For instance: when I referred briefly to revelations in history, I actually meant instances of faith in revelations. Such faith has great importance also in India and China, though it assumes very different forms there. But when I speak of the revelation of the truth by sudden illuminations in history, the term may give rise to misunderstanding: here I do not mean revelations of God, but unforeseeable manifestations—which cannot be deduced post facto as historically necessary—symbols, insights, motives, on the basis of which human life has been determined.

9. Personal Recollection and Motivation

In the field of the undemonstrable, every kind of thinking has a personal character. This is not a disadvantage; rather, it characterizes truth whenever it does not reflect individual caprice, and when the subjectivity has been sufficiently moved to assume the form of a universal idea. For this reason I shall briefly develop the few remarks about you included in my lecture. If I may, I shall take the liberty of addressing you personally. For this rejoinder I chose the form of the letter, so as to make at least a beginning to conversation. However, genuine communication is scarcely possible in public.

You complain about a number of my judgments, scattered in my lecture, and you quote the most provoking of them at the beginning of your reply. In this way, these sentences, picked out and brought together, acquire a massiveness that makes me appear in an unfavorable light. You say that an answer to them is impossible. This seems to me entirely true. Such judgments are intended to draw attention by their sharpness in the context of a general exposition, but should not be regarded as absolutely valid in themselves.

It seems to me that you, for your part, do not entirely avoid passing such judgments. You say that my remarks have little in common with the spirit of genuine communication; that I elude the hermeneutic problem; that a genuine dialogue cannot take place when "the opponent's intentions are ignored," as I ignore yours. "I have the impression," you write, "that Jaspers thinks it impossible to have a genuine dialogue with me, on account of what he calls my orthodoxy." These judgments concerning my offense against communication touch on a feature that is essential to my philosophizing—the will to communication. If your judgments are correct, my discussion of your concept of demythologization is not faithful to the spirit of my philosophy. The fact that I make "*ex cathedra* pronouncements," as you say, is in effect a negation of my philosophy. You know very well that this judgment is a blow at the very heart of my philosophy.

To this, I would reply as follows. First: Please, reflect that my lecture was not primarily meant as a communication to you personally. I was invited by a group of theologians, to speak in public about a group of ideas which you had advanced in theology to great effect, and about the spiritual soil on which those ideas seemed to have developed, that is to say, about that aspect of your personality which seemed inseparable from those ideas. My lecture was not an act of communication. It seems to me that it should not be judged from that point of view.

Second: Even in the realm of communication, radical characterizations seem to me one legitimate means among others. I shall not hold against you the fact that you charge me with negating my philosophy in practice: I cannot reply to this any more than you can reply to my judgments. Rather, I should have wished for even more outspoken judgments of that kind. For if such judgments do not spring from ill-will (I hope that such is not the case with my judgments, either), they are, even when they are erroneous, unfair, and exaggerated, a stimulus to the reader as well as to the person who is judged, to probe further. The attention is caught, even if the light does not shine squarely on the intended object. I have always found unfavorable judgments useful, for even when they spring from ill-will, they may contain a grain of truth. Our worst enemies can be helpful to us. But I do not think that such observations apply to us. At all events, you reply to me in a tone which, for all its intellectual opposition, has not forsaken kindness. I hope the same may be said of mine.

Finally, may I reply to your charge of non-communication with a personal recollection? When vital ideas are at stake, I believe one may run the risk of appearing inconsiderate. Conventional courtesy and impersonal matter-of-factness are out of place on such occasions.

When you have the impression, and state, that I do not believe a genuine dialogue between us possible, and this on account of the claim to exclusive truth laid by the revealed faith, I am frightened. What you say is true, and yet I refuse to believe that it is. It is true in so far as it is accounted for by the claim to exclusivity, and yet it should not be true in so far as it involves you and me. I chose your concept of demythologization as my subject for two reasons. The first was my intellectual anger against an alliance between demythologization and an orthodoxy that has maintained that the idea of God without Christ is madness from the Christian (i.e., also from your) point of view. Did you realize when you wrote the sentence (in *Studium generale* reprinted in *Glaube und Verstehen,* Vol. II) that in attacking the very heart of the philosophizing which I have attempted under the guidance of Plato, Plotinus, Spinoza, and Kant, you condemn the whole enterprise as madness? Certainly not, for you probably did not think of me at all. However, I was not affected personally, but as a philosopher. Angered by your complete unfamiliarity with philosophy, I was at the same time delighted with the blunt directness of your approach. For it encouraged me, and still encourages me, to be just as direct in my questions and judgments, and to concentrate on essentials. It is no doubt true that neither the great philosophers whom I revere, nor I myself, have personally encountered the godhead. But the godhead is present and all-encompassing, not as a mere idea, but actually. Is this madness?

The second reason for my choice, however, was the fact that for many decades I have been intellectually in communication with you, though this communication has been onesided. During the 1920's, you came to Heidelberg on one occasion and gave a lecture which both Dibelius and I admired. I also heard you preach at the Peterskirche. I was amazed by the orthodox, conventional content of your sermon, which did not accord with the spirit of your lecture. Later, when you were good enough to call on me, I asked you a few questions. You have no doubt forgotten all that. I was upset for a long time after your visit. I saw you as an unshakable rock of granite. My liking for you had begun when, as a boy, I noticed you in the school yard of the Oldenburg gymnasium (you were a few years younger than I). I abstained from seeking your acquaintance. I saw your shining eyes, and was glad that you existed. And later, during your visit to Heidelberg, I experienced the impossibility of making contact with you, an experience which became symbolic to me, and for which I held your orthodoxy responsible. Then I wrote down these sentences, which I later supplemented on the basis of other experiences, and which I used in my *Philoso-*

phischer Glaube (p. 61): "Discussion with theologians always breaks off at the crucial point. They fall silent, make an incomprehensible statement, speak of something else, assert something unconditionally, address kind and friendly words to one, without having actually realized what one has previously said—in the last analysis they are not really interested . . ."

In attacking your concept of demythologization I was motivated by both objective and personal considerations. Your concept of demythologization does not reflect a mere accident of personal opinion, but something that I, from my point of view, judge to be an evil, all the more because it has affected a man and scientist of your caliber. My lecture was actually a reply to your statement about madness. Therefore, the target of my criticism was orthodoxy, rather than demythologization.

If the foregoing personal remarks should once again appear to you as "*ex cathedra* pronouncements," I beg you to be indulgent, keeping in mind that speaking in apodictical statements can hardly be avoided when one wishes to be brief and clear; and I make the reservation that my apodicticity is not meant absolutely but only as a challenge. It can be dispensed with only in oral discussion, when our shuttling back and forth between arguments and counter-arguments nullifies, through its movement, what appears momentarily to be apodictic; it can also be dispensed with in irony, when by keeping all the propositions in a kind of suspense, we leave it up to our reader or our listener to feel the truth—a procedure for which I lack the talent.

10. *Conclusion*

In conclusion, it would be desirable to say something about the importance of the subject of our discussion in the present state of the world. This may disclose a deeper community between

us. True, questions of faith are in a sense more vital than anything that is merely topical. Yet they are put to the test only in
real life, in the present. Seen in this light, the scope of our discussion appears to be limited, but it acquires a specific importance.

By no means do I yield here to a modern inclination for world-
historical perspectives. No one knows whither we are going.
The total prognoses and the historical-philosophical interpretations of our epoch often trouble our minds; the Gnostic expecta-
tion of a historical process completely corrupts our reason. But
if we cannot know whither world history moves, we nevertheless
can outline possible perspectives for our orientation. Independently of an allegedly triumphant knowledge of the direction of
world history, we can be unswerving in our resolve to live according to our beliefs.

All of us today know about the conflict between freedom
and totalitarianism; yet few of us keep in mind that our vital
decisions and their order of importance are affected by this
conflict. All of us know of the political reality of these world-
encompassing powers; yet few of us are clearly aware of the
fact that this reality penetrates everywhere. All of us know that
we live in a transitional moment, sometimes disquietingly calm,
under the threat of destruction by unprecedented weapons; yet
few of us, it would seem, draw the necessary consequences from
this fact in our everyday awareness.

In such a situation, the subject of our discussion perhaps
carries little weight. It seems to be no more than a belated echo
of earlier struggles. Today, the old struggle over Christian or
Biblical truth has no more value, perhaps, than that of exempli-
fying human possibilities, which may be studied for the purpose
of clarifying real issues in our struggle for freedom.

Our situation today is in a sense comparable to that of the
Near East long ago when it was facing the enormous danger of
the all-destructive Assyrian. But today we have no prophets

capable of effecting a transformation of our life, our faith, our hope, and our action. Instead, we have only our Biblical tradition. The question is, What is it developing into?

Today the Biblical faith is doubted by millions of people. To millions of others it is becoming ever more unfamiliar. Where this is all leading, no one knows, in this connection any more than in others. Possibly the religious world is approaching its end. But it is also possible that the Biblical faith will become a power of the first rank. We may reflect on such possibilities as we strive to understand by what truth we live, and to live by it.

The Biblical faith in the form it has assumed in the churches has proved unreliable in crucial moments. If it is to mold the men who steer the course of history, it will do so in some new form which, for the time being, is still hidden. There is no point in reflecting on what can be brought about only by living men of faith. But our reflections on faith and philosophy have some bearing on this.

The Christian denominations seem today to be in this predicament. The power of the Catholic world grows irresistibly. Its kinship with totalitarianism, for all its tremendous differences from it, permits of comparison only in the sense that the free world must resist today, as it has in the past, the single rule of the Catholic church. But if the choice were only between Marxian and Catholic totalitarianism, the Catholic one would be infinitely preferable on account of its spiritual contents and its Biblical tradition, and of the explosive materials preserved in the Bible.

If the Protestant form of the Biblical faith is to survive—not for the sake of Protestantism but for the sake of freedom—the perspective is twofold. The Protestant opposition to myth and imagery, to the celebration of life in all its phases, results in weakening the hold of Protestantism on the masses. The greatness of Protestantism—its imageless decisions, its faith in transcendence, its austere depth—achieves reality only in exceptional individuals. The strength of Protestantism lies in the possible emergence of such men, who translate into action the great moral earnestness, the sobriety, and the nobility of political insight inherent in this faith.

Therefore, it seems to make no sense for the Protestant world to develop the forms of worship, the hierarchical structure, and the central administration of Catholicism. Such a course, though possibly desirable from another point of view, would lead ultimately to union with the Catholic Church.

Also the return to the "Word," to the attitude of Luther or Calvin, seems to me a sterile act of spiritual violence, which affects small groups without getting any further. My polemic bears on this point.

I see hope in the liberal faith, i.e., in Protestantism proper, which as such is capable of transforming the Biblical faith in all its manifestations. In this respect, as in others, no one can plan ahead. But freedom, moved by the pneuma of faith in God, projection of transcendence in the world, opens horizons, dissolves every veil, looks reality squarely in the eye, and arrives at decision with the natural certainty of reason. This freedom is also a condition for the survival of political freedom.

The subject of our polemic seems to me connected with the fate of freedom in the world, and the latter with the future of Protestantism.

But history, our destiny, and our responsibility must not be regarded as the ultimate criteria, either. What the individual actually is in his historicity, in the eternity of the moment, transcends history; at the same time, he helps to determine its course. And he is encouraged and confirmed by the truth he finds in the inexhaustibly profound writings of three millennia, one of the most irreplaceable of which is the Bible.

For all that I have attacked some of your ideas, you share with me a common opposition to totalitarianism in every form. Apart from my unintentional errors, my attack would be unjust if this agreement between us, which is so crucial today, were to be forgotten. After all, despite its sharpness, our dispute is not as radical as that between good and evil. Our agreement in the face of the totalitarian threat means more than any differences between us. I wish I had made myself clearer on this point.

Basel, April 1954   *Yours, Karl Jaspers*

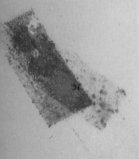

A LETTER TO KARL JASPERS
FROM RUDOLF BULTMANN

MY DEAR MR. JASPERS:

Thank you for your open letter. Today I must confine myself to expressing my pleasure in encountering a will to communication. I cannot at present discuss your letter in detail, nor can I say whether I will do it by a direct reply, or await the opportunity to come to grips with your ideas in another context.

Yours, Rudolf Bultmann